MILLION DOLLAR
AUTOS

MILLION DOLLAR
AUTOS

THE WORLD'S MOST EXPENSIVE AUTOMOBILES

GORDON CRUICKSHANK

Continental R

CHARTWELL
BOOKS, INC.

A QUINTET BOOK

Published by Chartwell Books
A Division of Book Sales, Inc.
110 Enterprise Avenue
Secaucus, New Jersey 07094

This edition produced for sale in the U.S.A., its
territories and dependencies only.

ISBN 1-55521-798-2

This book was designed and produced by
Quintet Publishing Limited
6 Blundell Street
London N7 9BH

Creative Director: Richard Dewing
Designer: Stuart Walden
Project Editor: Stefanie Foster
Editor: Sam Merrell
Picture Researcher: Mirco De Cet

Typeset in Great Britain by
Central Southern Typesetters, Eastbourne
Manufactured in Hong Kong by
Regent Publishing Services Limited
Printed in Singapore by
Star Standard Industries Private Ltd

CONTENTS

Introduction

Once upon a time, small boys would ask the driver of an exotic car "How fast does it go, mister?", but today they are more likely to ask "What's it worth?" A fine car has been an obvious expression of its owner's status and wealth since Edwardian days, when Mercedes and Rolls-Royce showed that the "horseless carriage" had developed into a refined and desirable means of transport. Since those early years, from being the sole preserve of the wealthy, car ownership gradually became more affordable to more people, thanks to the "people's cars" produced by Ford in the USA, Fiat in Italy, Citroën in France, and Austin and Morris in Great Britain. Today practically every family now owns a car which is a technically better vehicle than a luxury limousine of the 1930s.

The huge gap between an ill-equipped, 30 mph (48 kph) light-car and an 80 mph (129 kph) limousine, boasting brocade and sterling silver trimmings, has vanished. Any car in today's showrooms will cruise at 80 mph (129 kph) for hours, stay dry and warm in bad weather, and run for thousands of miles without attention. It was for such technical qualities, which we now take for granted, that the wealthy bought Rolls-Royces or Hispano-Suizas before the war, and not just for luxury and ostentation.

Standards are still increasing, and quality still takes time and effort to ensure, which is always reflected in the showroom price. In this book we have focused on the fastest, the finest, and, inevitably, the most expensive machines. Cars that most people will rarely see, let alone sit in or even drive. We cover not just the "superstars" of today, but also some of the rarest and most beautiful automobiles from all periods, including racing cars, which have become as desirable as great works of art. Fine cars, however, also provide the intoxicating thrill of being at the wheel, and so offer a combination of both physical and visual pleasure.

In the modern era it is the sports car, more than any other car, that is the mobile billboard of wealth. Today's limousines from Rolls-

Royce and Mercedes, though magnificently comfortable to ride in, have standard, mass-produced bodies in sober colours. Individuality has switched from luxury to overt speed, and once again it is possible to spend 10 or even 20 times the cost of a family car on a four-wheeled toy. A rich car enthusiast can now choose from a dozen cars capable of 200 mph (322 kph). Although there is barely a country in the world where this is allowed what counts is that everyone knows the car's potential.

Limited Editions and Speculation

It was during the boom years of the 1980s that the car became not only an essential fashion accessory, but also a seemingly gold-plated investment. The manufacturers realized that as long as the car was exciting enough there was almost no limit to what people would pay for it. Then even the maker's price-tag became irrelevant. Limited-edition cars appeared, for no practical reason except their own exclusivity. These began to be traded like stocks and shares, in some cases even before they were built. Speculators put their names down for a Porsche 959 or Ferrari F40, and then sold their place in the queue within weeks for a price well above the initial deposit. It became almost a point of honour to boast of how much over the odds a buyer had paid for a particular car. While prices rose, it made sense to enjoy the money rather than leave it in the bank!

Old cars, too, suddenly became sought-after items. Anything over 30 years old was liable to be labelled "vintage", which is likely to infuriate owners of the pre-1931 vehicles that actually qualify for the term. There is also no accepted definition of a "classic", which really ought to indicate a fine car of special significance – a high-point of its time – but is often carelessly used to label anything still running after 10 years. However, market forces soon sort out the high-flyers from the also-rans, and as the big international auction houses developed their specialist automobile departments the "good", or at least fashionable, machines became the stars. Over and over again the auction price "record" would be broken by a Bugatti, Ferrari or Aston Martin. This would pull up the prices of everything else sold in their wake, and so allow larger and larger profits to be made in shorter and shorter periods.

The profit-orientated 1980s led to radical changes in the world of vintage and classic cars. It had been a connoisseur's field

In an era when relative newcomers to car-making are able to build astonishingly fine cars, marketing departments think nothing of inventing new "prestige" names. Some, however, carry a pedigree which needs no advertising.

occupied by those who appreciated the elegance and engineering of old machinery, and who were prepared to struggle to keep their obsolete cars running, often to the puzzlement of the general public. All this changed, slowly at first and then increasingly quickly, to a mad scramble to buy any interesting car over 20 years old.

Auction sales proliferated, and they were held at more and more glamorous venues. Sales at stately homes and in the grand halls of Paris and Monaco became the gathering places of the fashionable and wealthy. Clutching thick, glossy catalogues and with their talk of "provenance" and "patina" they approached the auctions as they would a fine art sale. Although this market, like all others, has levelled out dramatically, vintage car gatherings are still places to be seen, preferably at the wheel of something fast and rare. Post-Impressionist paintings and Louis-Quatorze furniture are all very well, but you can't easily take them out and show them off in public.

All this feverish speculation has had both good and bad effects. Prices that doubled and redoubled squeezed out the ordinary enthusiast, while there were some buyers who neither knew nor cared much about their new purchases. They either sold on for quick profits or, worse, embalmed the car in an air-conditioned garage. A particular aspect of a car and one of its attractions, is that it needs to be used in order to preserve it properly. To treat it like an untouchable work of art is both pointless and potentially damaging. Fortunately, there were also buyers, perhaps initially drawn by the chic appeal, who were or became knowledgeable and enthusiastic owners, and brought their cars out to use on the road and the track.

Equally, rising car values helped the hobby as a whole. Specialist manufacturers found that it was worth their while to make small numbers of parts for rare cars. Damaged machines, which once would have been written off, became worth repairing. Derelict chassis, once destined to rust and rot away, became the starting point of major restorations. Notwithstanding the constant disputes over the originality of many of these rebuilds, the old-car hobby is healthier now than ever before. Led by the Mille Miglia retro event, classic tours are increasingly common, some offering merely beautiful scenery and an appreciative audience, while others recreate the pressure and risks of road-racing as it used to be. If you have a fine vintage or classic car, a rapid dash through the countryside with the prospect of a good lunch ahead is an excellent way to use it, especially for those uninterested in racing.

Even vintage racing has benefited from the upheavals of the 1980s. Many owners were reluctant to race a machine worth $54,000 (£30,000) if a big accident could cost the same amount to repair. If that same car, however, becomes worth $450,000 (£250,000), against a potential rebuilding cost of $72,000 (£40,000) or $90,000 (£50,000), you might as well get out and drive it – you just can't do that much damage.

Even if you own one fine old car, or a collection of 50, you still need an everyday motorcar. In that case, or if you have no interest in old machinery but still want something with style, you can go straight to Ferrari, Lamborghini and Bugatti in Italy, Porsche and BMW in Germany, or Aston Martin and Bentley in Britain. After the oil scares of the 1970s, when powerful cars seemed doomed to extinction, the resurgence of the specialist car has dominated the motoring industry. Every hatchback comes in a GTi version, and every driver dreams of graduating to a Porsche or a Ferrari. Only a very few, however, will ever take the wheel of one of the current breed of placid, reliable, easy-to-drive but sensationally fast supercars, which can reach speeds of 170 mph (273 kph) or more.

If you feel that such cars are a little impractical, or just not "different" enough, there are many firms who will tune and retrim anything on four wheels; starting from a Mini and going right up to a luxury saloon. There is nothing actually wrong with an £89,000 Mercedes 600SEL, but for the man who hates to drive anything "standard" it can be supercharged, restyled, and fitted out with marquetry and electronics until Mercedes themselves wouldn't recognize it. Although coach-built bodies on separate chassis have virtually ceased to exist, there are still "scratch-builders" who will create a unique car from the ground up. The cost is likely to be exorbitant, and it won't be a car for everyday use, but the price of individuality is sometimes more than mere money.

An optimist might say that the range and availability of exciting cars is greater now than ever before. Whether we will be able to continue enjoying them in the years to come is hard to predict, considering the environmental problems that face us and the diminishing fuel supplies. As the oil wells dry up and the price of petrol spirals, running a car may perhaps become an élite pastime once again. It may not be the cost of buying an interesting car, but the expense of feeding it with petrol that will make motoring a true luxury, a sport for millionaires only.

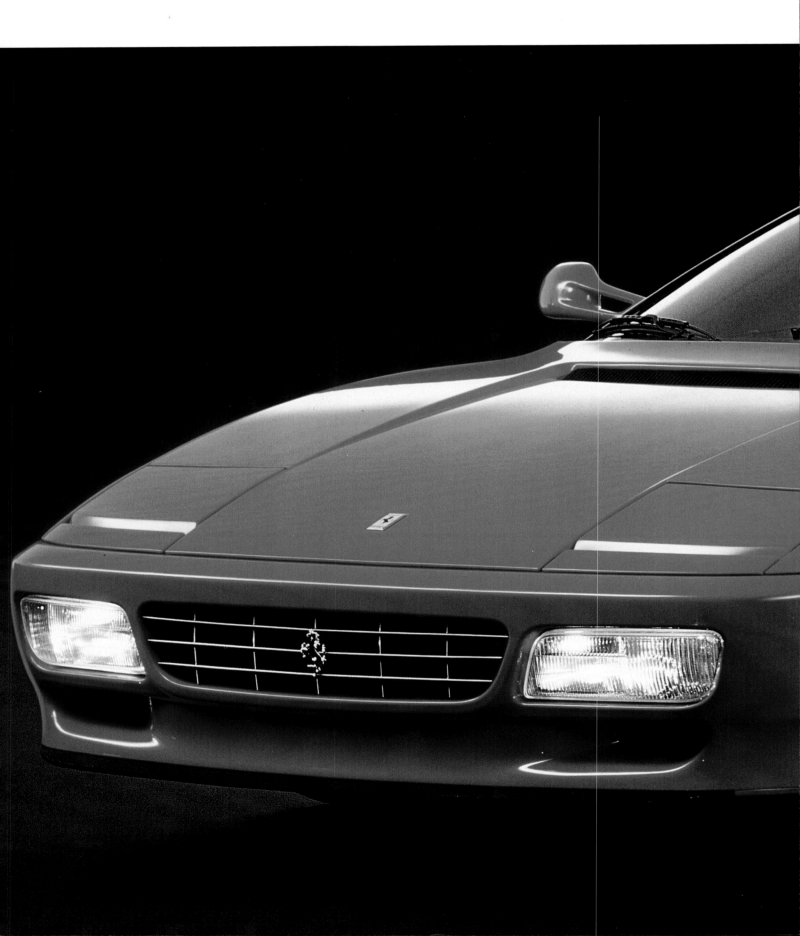

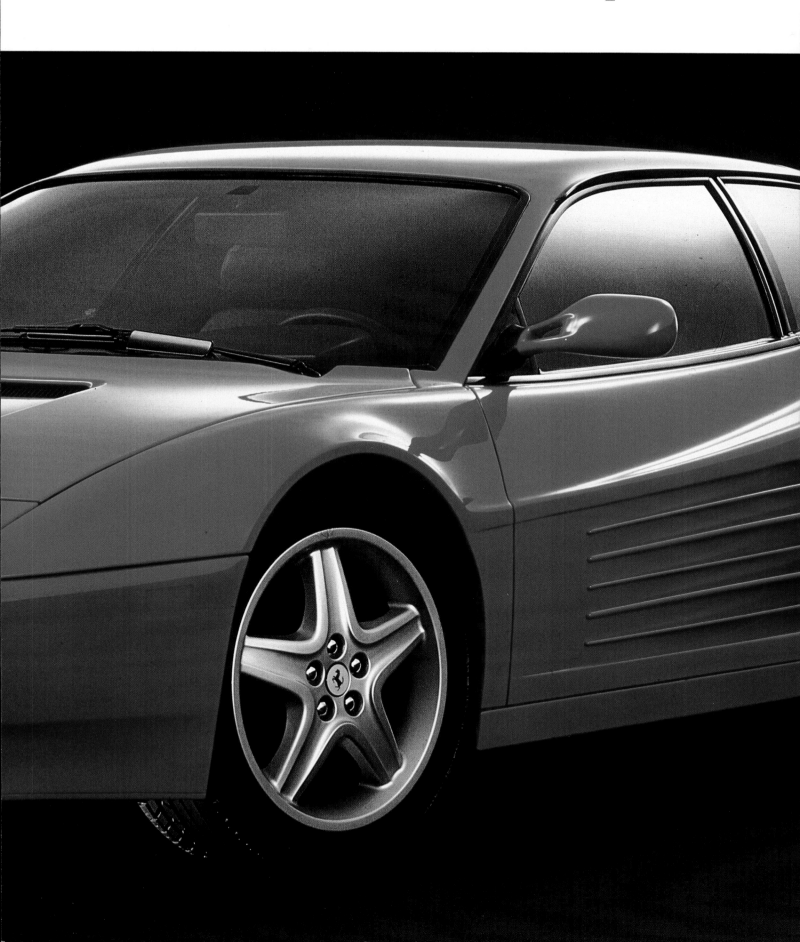

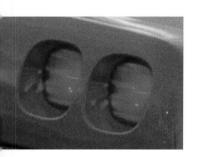

These are the cars that all schoolboys, and most grown men, dream of. The sort of cars that feature in the most indulgent of what the car magazines call "drive-stories". The cars that, though far from commonplace, are more likely to be seen and heard on the road than some of those included in this book. Cars whose names everyone knows, whether a car enthusiast or not. Names with Italian glamour, such as Ferrari and Lamborghini, with traditional mystique, like Aston Martin and Bentley, or names synonymous with technological excellence, such as Porsche. Most of these manufacturers have founded their glory on racing success. Driving a car with a racing connection is a powerful boast, and virtually essential to the image of

all sports cars from the 1920s until the 1960s. Within this period, sports car racing actually involved cars which could be driven on the road, from Bugattis and Amilcars up to the dual-purpose Ferraris of the early 1960s, such as the 250GT SWB and the even more extreme GTO.

But as the sports cars competing at Le Mans – the best-known arena – grew more specialized, it became increasingly difficult for private owners to buy such a GT car, drive it to race meetings, compete and then drive home. By 1965 the GT-class cars were unable to compete with the sports-prototypes at most races. The Ferrari 250LM, a surprise winner at Le Mans that year, was the last competitive car that could realistically be driven on public roads. Although the

1966 winner, Ford, did build a small number of road-going GT40s, known as the MkIII. But the 330P3 Ferrari, Ford MkIV and Porsche 910, which were the winners in this area of racing in 1967, were racing cars pure and simple. Never again would a major sports car race be won by a roadworthy car. Radically tuned engines, unforgiving clutches, and "cigarette-packet" ground clearance confined them to the race circuit only.

The breaking of this link meant that success in racing became less important to a sports car's attraction. Fast road cars developed into more comfortable machines, quieter, smoother and often air-conditioned, such as the Ferrari Daytona, Porsche 911 and Aston Martin DBS. Yet oddly, it was the maker with virtually no competition history, Lamborghini, who brought the racing-car's mid-engined balance to the showroom. The Miura, introduced in 1966, was the first high-profile sports car to make use of this layout. It brought ever-higher levels of road-holding, but in return for diminished practicality, poorer visibility and more critical handling characteristics.

Nevertheless, the fastest cars today (those that reach 180 mph (290 kph) or more) place their engines behind the driver and ahead of the rear wheels. With 400 bhp or more, the traction given by mounting the engine over the driven wheels is vital to prevent the car becoming wayward in slippery conditions. There are exceptions though, such as the rear-engined 4WD Porsche 959 and certain tuned versions of the Chevrolet Corvette. The Corvette's front-engined V8 recipe has matured over the years into a sophisticated chassis with exceptional grip, and some 380 bhp in its most powerful, quad-cam, 32-valve, Lotus-developed form, the ZR1. When turbocharged by firms like Callaway in the USA, it becomes the only front-engined member of the 190 mph (306 kph) club. On the other hand, its remarkably good value, like the Lotus Esprit, keeps it out of the exclusive circles filled by Lamborghini and Ferrari, even if it is just as fast.

The Lamborghini Diablo

In many ways, the Lamborghini Diablo has an unassailable position in terms of visual presence. It broadly follows the proportions of its predecessor, the Countach, which was a breakthrough in automotive styling. Before this astonishing shape appeared in 1971, bodylines were steadily lowering, making it more and more difficult to blend the cabin area, or "glass-house", elegantly into the profile. What the designer Marcello Gandini of Bertone did was to remove any break or interruption between the bonnet line and windscreen for the first time on a production car. The front edge of the Countach swept up almost straight to the screen-rail. Its far-forward driving position gave it a screen angle that was just about the lowest acceptable for visibility. This one-piece, wedge profile was obviously carried over into today's Diablo, and remains an ultimate in styling; overall car height has bottomed out, and no new design could practically undercut Gandini.

Under its striking skin, the Diablo has the specification to fulfil the dreams of the admiring bystanders, which it inevitably attracts. Ferruccio Lamborghini's intention when he started the sports car arm of his industrial business in 1963 was effectively to out-Ferrari Ferrari, and this meant also choosing a V12 to match the Maranello cars.

GUILLOTINE DOORS

The other winning feature of both the Countach and Diablo is the outrageous guillotine door, which pivots vertically from its front edge. It is debatable whether such a door actually improves access to this cramped machine, but the ability to drive around with both doors open certainly scores points for presence. Perhaps only Bertone's Stratos HF (the show car) has employed an even more dramatic way of entering a car – the driver stepped in through a hinge-up windscreen.

ABOVE: *Its stunning looks apart, the astonishing door mechanism always draws attention when someone steps out of a Diablo. By hinging on one corner, they allow access to this wide car in the tightest of parking spots.*

BELOW: *Automotive music: the melodious thunder of the Lamborghini's 12 cylinders volubly proclaims that here is a thoroughbred, while the beautifully finished castings show the skill that goes into its construction.*

BOTTOM: *With the gearbox between the seats, the stubby gear-lever has a crisp, positive feel. Lie back on the soft leather upholstery and the controls are ideally placed; high-speed travel demands a relaxed driving position.*

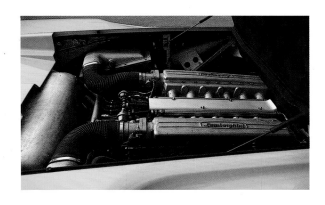

Since then a V12 has always powered the fastest cars from the Sant' Agata factory. Constant development has seen the capacity rise to the current 5.7 litres, with four valves per cylinder, fuel injection and an impressive 495 bhp. Power like this catapults the Diablo from 0–60 mph (0–97 kph) in 4.2 seconds, and to 100 mph (161 kph) a bare 4.3 seconds later. Keep the accelerator flat through third, fourth and into fifth, and a brave driver can prove the factory's top speed claim of an astounding 202 mph (325 kph), topping the Porsche 959 (197 mph/317 kph) and Ferrari 512TR (194 mph/312 kph). It is the fastest catalogued and homologated production car, but still not the fastest that can be bought.

Speeds like these become something of a numbers game played between the various factories, as virtually no customer will ever be able to stretch his car to the limits. Indeed, outside top-level racing circles, few people have the skill to do so even on an empty test-track. Reading the brochure figures is as close as most people get to experiencing the exhilarating limit of a car's performance, and the makers know that image is all-important. Buyers, choosing amongst cars at this sort of price level, may be tipped one way or the other by just a few decimal points, which make all the difference as they strive for one-upmanship.

The Diablo inherits the Countach's unique engine/transmission layout. Lamborghini designer Paulo Stanzani went from one unique layout to another, switching the 60-degree V12 from the Miura's transverse orientation (still never duplicated with a V12) to a longitudinal and "back to front" position in the new car. Normal racing procedure puts the clutch at the rear end, with the gearbox projecting behind the differential and half-shafts. The Diablo engine, however, drives forwards to a clutch and five-speed gearbox by the driver's elbow, from where a transmission shaft runs back through the block under the crankshaft to a differential just behind the engine. Apart from spreading the weight distribution evenly and bringing more weight to the front of the car (mid-engined machines are notoriously light at the front), it also means that the gear-lever engages the shift mechanism directly without the need of shift rods in the box. This reduces weight and produces a lighter, swifter change. It also improves access to the timing belts, distributor and alternator, which are situated in the rear instead of in the front as normal.

Drawbacks include the weight of the drive-shaft – non-existent in other central-motor systems – and a higher centre of gravity as a result of the engine having to clear the shaft. It does, however, have another big advantage – four-wheel drive. With the drive already originating in the middle of the car, Lamborghini's designers have been able to install a front drive-shaft and differential to produce the four-wheel Diablo VT.

As Audi showed with its turbocharged Quattro, the first of the high-performance 4WD vehicles, such a system brings new levels of grip and therefore safety. The reduced risk of wheelspin, and the resulting possibility of losing control at high speeds, plus the addition of anti-lock brakes allow for a car with the power of the Diablo but which is far easier to handle in poor driving conditions. Although at a cost of as much as a luxury saloon over the more "conservative" two-wheel-drive Diablo, already listed at $280,000 (£156,000), only a very few can afford to feel that safe.

Production supercars manufactured in small numbers, such as the Diablo and Ferrari TR512, often rely on well-proven technology that is easy to hand-build, rather than the sophisticated construction techniques employed by racing car designers. Even in the 1990s Lamborghini and Ferrari continue to use steel tube chassis frames as they have since the 1960s, while mainstream manufacturers use the latest materials, such as Porsche's steel monocoques, or Honda's all-aluminium NSX supercar, and racing car designers invariably use carbon-fibre composites. But the new technologies are sneaking in to the Italian plants. Under its coat of deep gloss paint, the Diablo combines steel, aluminium and Kevlar composite panels over its steel structure. Suspension under the Diablo consists of cast alloy double wishbones at each corner, with coil springs and firm dampers, which are able to absorb road impacts when cruising at more than 100 mph (161 kph).

Where the Ferrari F40 exposes the textured carbon-fibre of its fascia and floor, boasting of its competition car image, the Lamborghini retains the supple leather hides of a luxury car. The F40 owner sits in high-sided, carbon-fibre, competition seats between hollow doors with pull-cable releases, whereas the Diablo offers generous comfort and, of course, air conditioning. Compared to the older Countach, headroom, visibility and driving position are all improved. In the Diablo, a fast trip from Paris to Cannes is no longer an achievement, but a pleasure.

This is no effortless cruiser, however the heavy, sudden clutch and the metal-to-metal clunk of the gear-lever clicking through the

chromed gate require decisive control. The engine's instantaneous power delivery needs delicate application. Even at a massive 345/45 width, the rear tyres can be made to break traction with ease, and mid-engined cars, once they start to break away, are very difficult to catch. Specially developed Pirelli P-Zero rubber gives the Diablo the closest thing yet to a Formula One tyre for the road. They have three separate tread zones: on the inside, small blocks cope with wet conditions; a central stripe of slick rubber offers maximum traction and braking; while the fine tread on the outside shoulder gives immense cornering power on dry tarmac.

ABOVE: *Its name means "devil", and with its guillotine doors raised it's easy to see the Diablo's horns, or the fighting bull of Lamborghini's symbol.*

Ferrari's "Red-head" – Testarossa

Although not quite as extreme in styling, Ferrari's equivalent to the Diablo is just as dramatic on the road. With its straked gills down each flank, the Testarossa fired a new trend when it was revealed in 1984. By tapering the cabin in towards the tail and sweeping the wide rear arches up from the waistline to a flat deck over the huge tyres, the designers Pininfarina gave the car the look of a Group C sports car fresh from Le Mans. It was a bold idea, for the car is massively wide in any case, and the resulting rear view is, if anything, even more eye-catching than Diablo's.

Applying the Testarossa name reinforced the racing con-notations, and the name has clung to the car even though from 1992

BELOW: *Under those sweeping lines lies a flat-12 power-unit which can push the TR to 194 mph (312 kph) with stability and safety. And to match the performance the huge 18-inch wheels contain massive "race-bred" braking power.*

the improved and faster version became known simply as the 512TR. "Testarossa" graced several of Enzo Ferrari's greatest sports-racers in the 1950s. Literally meaning "red-head", it refers to the cylinder-heads of certain models that were painted red to differentiate them in the racing shop from similar, but less powerful units. The TR's cylinder heads are also scarlet, although the engine is of a different layout to any of the racing Testarossas. Instead of a powerful four or the glorious V12, a flat-12 "boxer" squats over the rear axle. To shorten the whole car, the gearbox and differential are directly under the block instead of behind it. As with Lamborghini's unconventional layout, this offers certain advantages of access, but places the weight of the engine rather high. Theoretically this would cause a more twitchy chassis, but the TR's levels of grip are so astonishingly high that only the very bravest driver is likely to find out.

Twin camshafts per bank and 48 valves extract a fearsome 421 bhp from the 5-litre engine at a rousing 6750 rpm, with Bosch Motronic engine management controlling the fuel injection and electronic ignition. However, unlike previous Ferraris, the TR's refinement has increased to the point where the wonderful noise of the engine working hard is insulated from those inside. The relentless acceleration and rock-solid stability are just as impressive, the steering is precise and alive, but the delicious background noise heard in the F40 or Diablo is muted in this car. On the other hand, the sensation of being pressed into the seats as the car streaks to 60 mph (97 kph) in 4.8 seconds makes up for it. Pushed all the way, Ferrari claims that the TR can notch up 194.5 mph (313 kph).

Ferrari also adhere to traditional construction techniques with the TR. They use a tubular frame with steel and alloy panelling, which is suspended on double wishbones and coil springs front and rear. Huge 18-in (46-cm) alloy wheels are clad in very low-profile rubber of 235/40 front and 295/35 rear, well able to absorb the muscular 360 foot-pounds of torque.

Thanks to their competition pedigree, Ferraris have in the past tended to have rather plain interiors. Even now, and despite the enormous price-tag, their interior appointments are not lavish. There is no polished wood, and only a selection of the electronic devices to be found in an S-class Mercedes or a Rolls-Royce. Electric windows, yes, but no power seats, and some of the detailing may be familiar from other cars. The high cost of tools to mould plastic is such that it makes sense for the Maranello plant to rely on the Fiat parts bin for

indicator stalks and control knobs. There is even a tradition of this, as Ferrari coach-builders have often bought small parts from the same sources for their cars.

Yet the old accusation of poor assembly have been banished in the new generation – quality materials abound. In front of the driver, the typically Ferrari instruments are double-banked in a high binnacle, neatly stitched in Connolly leather. This extends to most of the cabin as well as the fitted luggage, which is specially made to fit into the cramped luggage compartment in the nose, and boasts discreet, prancing horse (cavallino rampante) logos to create a subtle effect when carried into the hotel. Another trademark, the round black gearknob, sits above the exposed metal gate in which the slim lever moves. That, and the yellow cavallino rampante shield in the centre of the steering wheel, are the constant reminders to the lucky pilot of the heritage and potential of the machine; the reasons for spending $243,000 (£135,000) for the privilege of sitting there.

ABOVE: *Restrained comfort in the cockpit of the Ferrari 512TR; high-quality leather everywhere, and between the seats the famous ball gear-knob and exposed metal gate which have typified Ferraris since the 1950s.*

Aston Martin's Virage

There is a profound contrast between the machines from the level plains around Modena, and the sports cars built by Aston Martin Lagonda, deep in the English countryside of Buckinghamshire. Aston Martin, established for longer than either of the Italian marques, also has a history of distinction on the race-track, which includes winning Le Mans and the World Sports Car championship in the same year, 1959. Since the 1960s, though, the Newport Pagnell factory has built increasingly luxurious grand tourers. They have retained a front-engined layout and pride themselves on the hand-shaped aluminium bodywork, hand-sewn leather and beautifully crafted and figured wood inside the expansive cockpit. An Aston Martin is a paragon of comfort and exclusivity.

These cars, though big in all dimensions, have the performance to match. Since 1972, all models have been powered by a quad-camshaft V8, whose size and output has risen steadily. Today's 5.4-litre Virage packs 330 bhp under its long bonnet and pushes 350 foot-pounds of torque through its rear wheels, which is enough to propel the two-seater coupé up to 155 mph (250 kph). Aston Martin also usually has something extra to offer its keenest customers, and for the Virage it consists of a conversion package that boosts the power output by no less than 40%.

Once this conversion has been carried out, the capacity of the 48-valve engine jumps to a giant 6.3 litres. Gas-flowed cylinder heads, uprated injection settings and a hotter camshaft combine to extract a massive 465 bhp, while the torque leaps to 460 foot-pounds. This abundance of muscle pushes the Virage's peak-speed up to 174 mph (280 kph), and half a second is shaved from the 0–60 (0–97) time, paring it to 5.5 seconds. Even more dramatically the 6.3 Virage can touch 100 mph (161 kph) in a little over 11 seconds.

To slow the beast, Aston's engineers employ the largest brake discs ever fitted to a production car; at 14 inches in diameter, they are virtually as big as a complete Mini wheel. Surrounding them are 18 in (46 cm) alloy wheels clad in 285/45 ZR Goodyear Eagle tyres. Like most supercars, the Virage relies on double wishbone suspension at the front, but unusually it has a De Dion rear axle located by a Watts linkage. Its excellent road-holding blends with its overall more relaxed character, as compared to its mid-engined fellows. For instance, it also has power steering and may be ordered with an

automatic gearbox. Yet this grand tourer is no mere boulevard cruiser. The ride is firm, the steering response taut and the acceleration sensational. To drive the Virage fast on open roads takes skill and accuracy, and negotiating it through traffic needs care as the soft aluminium bodywork is easily dented. Considering that the 6.3 conversion alone costs $90,000 (£50,000), taking the car's total to $328,995 (£182,775) repairs are to be avoided if possible!

BELOW: Following a long line of powerful front-engined Grand Tourers, Aston Martin's Virage retains traditional interior appointments, while the shape of the famous Aston grille still adorns the nose.

RIGHT: *Despite its size and grandeur, the Continental R is astonishingly rapid and agile. Its 6.7-litre turbocharged V8 and tough automatic gearbox propel it to 60 mph (97 kph) in a mere 6.6 silent seconds.*

The Bentley Continental

Another car of a similar ilk, but with even greater exclusivity, comes from the Rolls-Royce stable. For many years a Bentley was merely a re-badged Rolls-Royce, which was a shameful and sad fate for a name with a once glorious past at Le Mans. In the 1980s, however, the Turbo was introduced, adding electrifying performance to Rolls-Royce luxury, and attracting the first royal customer for many years – Prince Charles. He keeps one alongside his Aston Martin Volante convertible. This is also the way Virgin tycoon Richard Branson prefers to travel, when not in one of his airliners. Then in 1991 the first pure Bentley for several decades appeared.

Called "Continental", after the long-legged touring coupés of the 1950s and 1960s, it boasts a turbocharged variant of the long-running RR V8 contained within sleek, two-door coupé bodywork. Its all-independent running gear derives from the luxurious Rolls-Royce Silver Spirit, stiffened and sharpened to Turbo R specification, giving a luxurious blend of comfort, adhesion and silence which almost no other car can approach. Electronic adaptive dampers give the heavy machine a sporting ride when it is driven hard, but relax their grip to maximize the magic carpet effect when merely cruising.

No manual gearbox car has rolled out of the Crewe works since the 1960s, and the Continental remains true to the tradition. This is first and foremost a luxury carriage, which also happens to be exceptionally fast. It does, however, have a four-speed automatic instead of the three-speeder of its more upright stable-mates which carry the Silver Lady. Rolls-Royce have long enjoyed being coy about the performance of their cars; to questions about horsepower or acceleration figures, the standard reply is that they are "adequate". In fact, this remarkable Q-car can reach 60 mph (97 kph) in 6.6 seconds, and 100 mph (161 kph) in an even more improbable 16 seconds.

Within the hushed cabin, the craftsmanship is of the highest level. There is Connolly leather, of course, and naturally figured walnut veneers. More impressive than this "standard" luxury is the sheer weighty quality of the smallest item. Ventilation grilles of cast metal, machined door-lock knobs, silkily sliding levers for the air-conditioning. Every detail works as though it has been individually bedded in – and it probably has. Creating cars with such skill and care is expensive, and Bentley expect to find fewer than 300 people a year who are able to write a cheque for $315,000 (£175,000) for a Continental.

THE BUGATTI EB110

They say money isn't everything, and if you want to be part of the renaissance of the revered Bugatti marque you will soon find that this is true. Despite the mystique that built up around his beautiful racing and sports cars before World War II, the company effectively died with its founder Ettore Bugatti in 1947. Forty years later, a business group bought the rights to the name and set to work on one of the most intense and talked-about new car projects ever. From a standing start they set to work on a supercar worthy of carrying the oval badge with the EB initials – the EB110.

A glorious name reborn; the new EB110 Bugatti outside the high-tech factory in Modena where these exclusive machines are built.

In a striking new factory outside Modena, the team started by designing a novel engine; a V12 with not one or two, but four turbo-chargers for instantaneous response. Aided by the turbo-chargers, the 3.5-litre, 60-valve unit spits out 550 bhp and can rev to 9200 rpm. Within the carbon-fibre composite chassis, the inline block is offset to the left with the six-speed gearbox alongside, driving all four wheels. Computer-controlled, semi-active suspension presses the Bugatti down to the road as the speed climbs. Its claimed maximum speed of 217 mph (349 kph) demands absolute stability. As for luggage space or a spare tyre – well, no. As a Bugatti engineer said half-jokingly, "if you have a car like this, you use your portable phone to call for help from your helicopter!"

Secrecy veiled the car's body design before its launch, and controversy has followed it since. Only the tiny horse-shoe opening on the nose recalls the famous pre-war radiator shape. The EB110 is a low, compact two-seater in the Lamborghini mould, rather than a front-engined fast tourer of Bugatti legend. Its unusual headlamp design certainly makes it distinctive, but not beautiful. However, its rarity, its name, and its extravagant speed had potential buyers offering deposits before either the shape or the price were revealed. But a Bugatti is not easily bought. Even if you feel that you can spare the startling cost, the company will want to know who you are. The acceptability of your bank balance is only the start, and may not be enough. They will want to know if you have social status, or are respectably famous, or if you have enough blue blood; only then may you be considered for a place on the waiting list. If you have all three, who knows, you might even be allowed to choose the colour.

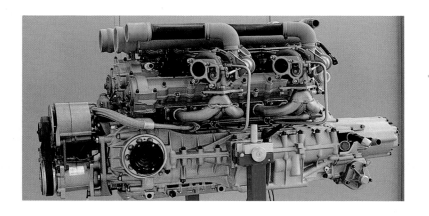

LEFT: *Boasting four turbochargers the Bugatti engine is not only unique, but also more flexible than most turbo units. Five tiny valves per cylinder can deal with speeds of 9,200 rpm and contribute to the prodigious 550 bhp output.*

ABOVE: *Bugatti also chose guillotine doors for its mid-engined masterpiece. Note the central insert in the grille, echoing the famous horseshoe radiator which graced all of Ettore Bugatti's cars.*

ABOVE: *Barely recognizable as a relative of the flat-six which has powered Porsches for 40 years, the twin turbos of the 959 raise the output to an awesome 450 bhp.*

Exclusivity has its own appeal. Some artefacts become scarce through time and by accident, but others are rare by design, because the makers have chosen to restrict the numbers to keep the value high. This calculated exclusivity applies to art prints, china plates, books, and, of course, motor cars. In the past some fine cars were produced in limited numbers because they were so costly, or un-popular, or built essentially for competition only. One of the revolutions of the 1980s has been the arrival of the "limited edition" car, which has buyers scrambling to put their names down before the first ex-ample has even been made. These cars are invariably extremely ex-pensive, but in a thriving investment market there are plenty of wealthy purchasers confident that they can enjoy the vehicle for a while and then resell at a profit. It's a long way from the traditional wisdom that says that fast cars are money down the drain.

Porsche 959

Porsche has an international reputation for unconventional but effec-tive engineering. In 1981 the Stuttgart firm amazed the automotive world with a prototype called the 959. Without abandoning the theme of the longest-running sports car of all, the 911, the company's Weissach development centre produced the fastest, most technically sophisticated, and most expensive car in the world, an all-wheel drive, 450 bhp sensation capable of virtually 200 mph (322 kph). It was the first of a new generation of supercars capable of doubling the magic "ton". The 959 achieved another double when it won the Paris-Dakar rally across Africa in 1986 and 1987 *and* raced at Le Mans a year later – the first "road-going" (albeit highly modified) sports car to do so for 20 years. A sudden change in the racing rules made it quickly redundant as a competition car, but that did not deter buyers. Nor did the price of $270,000 (£150,000), an unheard of sum at the time.

Porsche's engineers grafted water-cooled, four-valve heads and twin KKK turbo-chargers on to the venerable air-cooled flat-six engine design. A six-speed gearbox, positioned ahead of the block, drove both axles, but the company broke new ground with the control system. The torque split is electronically controlled by a computer, which reacts to many different factors to prevent any wheelspin in any conditions. Thanks to its "mountain-goat" traction, the 959 can streak from rest to 60 mph (97 kph) in an astonishing 3.9 seconds. Computers also control the dampers and even monitor the tyre pressures while the car is moving.

LEFT: *Desert raider: as well as racing at Le Mans, the 959 scored two successive victories in the punishing Paris-Dakar endurance rally across Africa.*

LEFT: *First of the few: initially intended as a homologation exercise for competition, the technology-crammed 959 became a high-profile success for Porsche.*

ABOVE: *Even the 959's wheels are advanced: electronic sensors monitor tyre pressure and a built-in inflation system tops them up when on the move.*

Above the waistline the 911 cabin is familiar, but the rest of the body is wider and smoother, with sensuous low-drag curves. Only 250 were built, and the price included a trip to Germany for a familiarization course at the Weissach test-track. Heavy demand and long delivery times caused resale prices to soar to three and four times the factory cost, even before the production run ended in 1990. The 959 was the car that proved that there was no price limit for a car as long as it was exciting and exclusive enough.

Ferrari F40

If it was Porsche who broke the ground for six-figure costs (in UK sterling) with the 959, it was Ferrari who really sowed the seed of the new crop. For its fortieth anniversary in 1986, Maranello took the wraps off a celebratory car. It was noisy, cramped, harsh and thirsty and it made a Testarossa look cheap. It was the F40, and it stole the crown of "the world's fastest car" for a while.

Stark and uncompromising, the F40 is built like a race car – though plans to race it at Le Mans never matured. Instead, it joined the club of 200 mph (322 kph) road cars, touching 201 when given its head. Hand-assembled on a carbon-fibre floorpan, the cabin is bare with no carpets, a plain grey dash, no radio, and just a wire pull for a door handle. Deep, moulded seats grip the occupants tightly, because this chassis can generate such strong G-forces that without them the driver would be in the passenger's lap on every left-hand bend.

Behind the driver, and completely uninsulated, the twin-turbo, 32-valve V8 snarls out a massive 478 bhp, filling the cockpit with an unmistakable yowl. It is enough to pull in the 60 mph (97 kph) tag at 4.8 seconds and tick off 100 (161 kph) before another four seconds has gone. Yet the 2.9-litre powerhouse is equally capable of handling city traffic – if the "crew" can stand the crashy, low-speed ride. Every part of an F40 is tuned to performing at speed, and the usual pot-holes in city streets reverberate through the flimsy Kevlar bodywork like grenades.

Once unleashed, though, the F40 offers one of the greatest motoring experiences of all. Road-roller tyres, 335/35 at the back, cling

BELOW: When Ferrari announced the gorgeous F40 there were plans to race it. Instead, it became the ultimate "must have" machine – the fastest road car in the world.

BELOW: *With its razor-sharp handling and slingshot acceleration, Ferrari's fastest son is a machine for very special journeys – minus luggage.*

like superglue, and the turbos effortlessly catapult the car forwards. Little wonder that there was an immediate queue to order one. From the beginning Ferrari never seemed sure how many they planned to build – 200, 400, 500 – but the orders kept coming in until 1,100 was reached. In fact the demand grew so strong that the car could be resold immediately for far more than the new price. At their peak, an F40 could jump from $354,600 (£197,000) at the factory gate to around $1080,000 (£600,000) in the time it took to be delivered to London,

Munich or Los Angeles. Buyers had to promise not to re-sell within a year, but many couldn't resist ignoring the small print.

Ferrari and Porsche had proved that in the booming 1980s price was no object. This opened new marketing areas for adroit manufacturers. Instead of investing millions in tooling up for mass production, requiring millions of cars to be sold to break even, they realized that they could hand-build a limited edition car and charge whatever it cost. A new strain of supercars was born.

RIGHT: *Lift the enormous Kevlar tail and the twin-turbo powerhouse is revealed. The massive perspex rear window is louvred to release the blast of heat produced.*

Jaguar's "Super-Cat"
The XJ220

Most observers were surprised when Jaguar, builders of conservative luxury cars, announced a four-wheel drive entrant to the 200 mph (322 kph) club. It would be called the XJ220, for 220 mph (354 kph) was the aim, eclipsing the Italians in one bound. It caused a sensation at the 1988 Motorfair in London, and buyers flocked to put down a £50,000 deposit without even knowing the final price. But then things went ominously quiet, and rumours spread that the XJ220 was cancelled, or it was nearly ready, or it was being re-designed.

At last, in 1990, a "new" XJ220 was exhibited. It was a smaller, neater, two-wheel drive car, equipped with a 3.5-litre twin-turbo V6 instead of the big V12. Not only had the first customers ordered without knowing the price, they had not even known what car they were getting. However, the revised car seemed to be a better design, which was good news after having waited for it for so long. The final bill, $522,000 (£290,000) without taxes, had risen with inflation and tax to not far off $720,000 (£400,000) in 1992.

ABOVE: *Despite its claim to be the fastest car in the world, Jaguar's svelte XJ220 pampers its occupants with air-conditioning, leather upholstery, and the smooth ride for which the Coventry marque is famous.*

RIGHT: *The oval grille recalls the E-type, but no Jaguar ever before offered 200 mph (322 kph) and air-conditioned luxury in a high-tech, low-drag package like this.*

ABOVE: *Another 200 mph (322 kph) Jaguar-powered supercar which offered a tempting gamble: the XJR-15 cost a million dollars, but customers stood to win it back in a high-profile race series.*

RIGHT: *Close cousin to the TWR Le Mans Jaguars, the 450 bhp XJR-15 clothes its composite chassis with a sensational shape – and it has the lights and accessories to make it road-legal.*

The XJ220 combines Jaguar tradition with technical advances. It has soft, rounded curves, an oval grille reminiscent of the immortal E-type, and – for the first time in a production Jaguar – a mid-mounted engine. Its construction is a first, with a bonded aluminium monocoque and an all-aluminium body. Trimmed for comfort, this air-conditioned super-cat aims squarely at the Lamborghini Diablo and 512TR market, and on paper beats them both for performance. With 500 bhp, it can reel off 60 mph (97 kph) in 4.0 seconds and its top speed has been clocked at 212 mph (341 kph) – a fraction short of its claimed goal, admittedly, but it would be churlish to complain.

The firm charged with bringing the XJ220 into production is JaguarSport, a joint-venture with Tom Walkinshaw Racing (TWR); the independent outfit which runs the successful Jaguar race effort. It was TWR who so radically altered the original overweight XJ220 concept. In 1990, while the faithful were still waiting for their XJ220s, they and the Jaguar management were surprised to be faced with a rival from TWR – a car with a mid-mounted Jaguar V12 and carrying the famous Jaguar name.

The JaguarSport XJR-15

TWR had all the facilities to build their own composite chassis for the Le Mans-winning XJR-series sports-racers, so a limited edition road car was relatively simple for them to develop. Their new offering was expensive but beautiful, and most important of all it was ready. More than one customer who had been too late to book an XJ220 switched to the new XJR-15, captivated by its sleek skin and its Group C pedigree. Not only did it look like a racing car, but each of the 30 buyers were guaranteed entry to a special race series in 1991 with a $1,000,000 prize. The price of a ticket was the cost of buying the car – $1,000,000. It was a spectacular gamble and a spectacular trio of races, which left two brothers owning a million-dollar car – for free.

The '15 compares more to a Ferrari F40 than a Lamborghini, with its bare Kevlar interior, cut-away steering wheel, and no protection from the noise of the 7-litre V12 behind the driver's head. Anyone brave enough to risk his half-million pound 200 mph (322 kph) machine in the traffic will come back exhilarated, but battered. Rock-solid suspension, a clutch requiring Schwarzenegger-like strength, razor-sharp chassis responses, and the relentless wail of 450 barely-silenced horsepower make this a car for the dedicated.

Aston Martin Zagato

Few discomforts afflict the owner of one of the 50 Aston Martin Zagatos. Inspired by the gorgeous lightweight DB4GT, which the Italian coach-builder Zagato bodied for Aston in 1961, the Newport Pagnell firm decided in 1985 to renew this successful association. The stripped-down and lightened floorpan of a V8 coupé was sent to Italy, where Zagato's stylists and engineers went to work. Their final design aroused spirited and heated argument; some felt it was unattractive and un-inspired, others that it was typical Zagato eccentricity. Whatever the opinion it was certainly unmistakable on the road, an eye-catching and ear-bending rarity with Zagato's "double-bubble" roof trademark.

Under the bulge of its bulbous bonnet are the four twin-choke Weber carburetters, which feed the Vantage, or high perform-ance, version of the quad-cam Aston V8. The 430 rousing horsepower can propel the alloy-bodied coupé to 186 mph (299 kph), but the cabin interior retains at least some of the comforts of its luxurious, fully-appointed brother. Shorter and lower than the Aston-bodied car, the Zagato is unashamedly a two-seater only – with a padded shelf instead of even token rear seats – but plenty of hand-stitched, top-quality leather maintains the sense of luxury. Only silence is absent as the throaty V8 snarl echoes through the cabin, audibly reminding the driver of the car's dramatic performance. It is agile, has terrific road-holding, and is a very rare sight on the road. Unfortunately, it tends

RIGHT: *Aston instrument panels have traditionally imitated the shape of the grille, and the Zagato respects that with the leather cowl that shades the polished veneer dash.*

to attract the attention of the police, as comedian Rowan Atkinson found after taking delivery of his bright-yellow example.

Yet again, buyers had snapped up all 50 before the first car was built, knowing that it was a solid-gold investment and that values would soar almost immediately beyond the initial cost of $156,600 (£87,000). Aston Martin insisted that there would only ever be 50 of them, which kept the value high, but a year later they brought out a convertible version. It was arguably more attractive and certainly more expensive at $171,000 (£95,000), and again it was limited to 50 examples. Today these are even more sought after than the original Zagato, fetching a premium over the "tin-top" version.

BELOW: *Zagato's angular re-interpretation of the famous Aston Martin grille was controversial, but the car was pure adrenalin on the road – two seats, 430 bhp, and the unmistakable howl of a hot V8.*

"SANCTION 2"

The limited-edition concept is exploited in a variety of ways. At one end is the small-scale assembly line, which, for instance, has turned out well over 1,000 Ferrari F40s, while at the other is another Aston Martin/Zagato project – the "Sanction 2". Not 50, not even 10, but only 4 of these exotic machines have been manufactured. They were built in 1991, but they are perfect duplicates of the 1961 model. The original was a Zagato-bodied competition version of the Aston Martin DB4GT, which are today immensely valuable. The new car, though, is not a look-alike, or a copy on modern running gear. It is, says Aston Martin, a resumption of the original production, authorized by the factory and using the correct DB4 mechanicals, which were sent to Italy and assembled by the same coachworks (and even by some of the same craftsmen).

Using the restored floorpan of the lightest and fastest variant of the DB4, which was a successful competition car in the early 1960s, Zagato's craftsmen clothe it in hand-shaped aluminium beaten over the original body jigs. Small components are matched from the same sources as 30 years before, and the end result is indistinguishable from the 1961 cars.

Even though all the parts are available, there is still one more element that sets this project apart from others – chassis numbers. In 1961, a total of 23 chassis numbers were allocated for DB4 Zagatos, but only 19 were built. It is those four "missing" cars that have now been built, 30 years behind schedule. The "Sanction 2" phrase signified that the project has the authority of the original makers.

Aston Martin and the idea's instigator Richard Williams, an Aston expert, stated that there would be no more, despite many approaches by collectors offering £500,000 or more. Even at that price it looks excellent value, considering it is more or less identical to the older car, and an original DB4 Zagato sold for $2.8 (£1.54) million in 1990 – buying the new one could be seen as a saving of one million pounds.

Clearly visible through the big wood-rimmed wheel, the DB4 GTZ's dials nestle in their distinctly Aston Martin fascia.

*Sanction 2:
possibly the most limited
edition ever was another
Aston/Zagato project.
Four examples have been
assembled 30 years after the
first 19.*

The Cizeta

Almost as rare as the "Sanction 2" Aston Martin, but with enthusiastic plans for growth, is another Italian supercar – the Cizeta. The car's name is simply derived from the initials in Italian of the man who conceived and developed it, Claudio Zampolli, and its home, like that of so many other supercars, is Modena. Like the renewed Bugatti company, Zampolli felt that it made sense to be close to the many specialist automotive firms located around the town. Not content with buying in established parts, he too has developed a completely new power-plant, backed initially by Giorgio Moroder, the rock musician. The Cizeta is not quite a 200 mph (322 kph) car, its top speed is a mere 190 mph (306 kph), but it is very special. Under the engine cover lies a unique mechanical sight – the only V16 motor in production today. A couple of pre-war, American luxury saloons (Cadillac and Marmon) and one or two racing cars (Auto-Union and BRM) have used this layout, but this is the first post-war production V16. It is the first such unit to appear in an outright sports car, and perhaps the most complex engine ever to reach the road.

Styled by Marcello Gandini – who also created the Diablo – the Cizeta V16T is in a similar mould, with a forward cabin and side windows sweeping down to the front wheels. Its aluminium body clothes a tubular steel chassis with an unusual transmission layout. The big engine sits sideways across the car, but the gearbox projects longitudinally behind, driven from the middle of the block. This effectively makes the engine two linked V8s, with four twin-cam cylinder heads, making eight camshafts, and an amazing 64 valves! 6 litres in capacity, with electronic ignition and fuel injection, it produces an awesome 520 bhp, with almost 400 foot-pounds of torque. To reduce the justifiable "green" criticism it is fitted with a catalytic converter.

Inside, the Cizeta takes the luxury route, with leather trim and a comprehensive climate-control system. Unusual large white instruments face the driver, and, for the driver who is determined to achieve that extra mile-per-hour, the rear-view mirrors can be programmed to retract automatically at a set speed. As each car is virtually hand-built, purchasers may choose the interior and exterior trim and fittings. But even for around $630,000 (£350,000) there is one accessory you just can't have. Zampolli does not believe a driver should smoke, and therefore this rare and expensive machine arrives without something even the meanest economy car has as standard – an ashtray.

BELOW: *Styled by Marcello Gandini, the Cizeta's striking shape is even rarer on the road than a Lamborghini. Aerodynamics are crucial for a car capable of over 190 mph (306 kph).*

LEFT: *Low, sleek and mean – the super high-tech Cizeta comes from Modena, Italy, the home of Bugatti and Ferrari, and Lamborghini's base is also close by.*

Today's mass-production has brought mass uniformity to our roads. Admittedly, the modern car is more efficient, reliable and practical, but at the cost of flexibility. In the pre-war days, having ordered a chassis, it was up to the customer to choose the body. The customer could select any one from a book of body designs, or commission one of the more creative coach-builders to come up with something unique and striking. Monocoque construction, and the mass consumption that goes with it, has removed that opportunity for individual choice. On virtually all the cars produced today, the body is the chassis and tampering with it is difficult.

But creativity still thrives and many people desire individuality to be added to their showroom cars, and there are specialist firms eager to comply. These modern equivalents of the coach-builder will create and engineer almost anything. They often begin by dismantling a brand-new, luxury car in order to rebuild its engine, interior and body-work. Whether the result is subtle and attractive – or downright outrageous – depends on the client's taste and wishes.

ABOVE: *Anything is possible! Panther of England converted this Mercedes 500 SEC coupé to "gull-wing" spec. Inside, white leather, walnut and a television – to the owner's "taste".*

Koenig GmbH

If you want the prestige of, for instance, a Mercedes, but you also want exclusivity and supercar performance, then the German firm Koenig can realize your dream. Their workshops can handle any special project that their rich clients may bring, but they are best known for their tough-looking and extremely fast Mercedes conversions. They have engine modifications and body conversions on offer for all the Stuttgart saloons, but at the top of the range is their reworking of the big coupé, the 500SEC. Popular with businessmen, this model also appeals to film stars and the first Koenig SEC completed was for Sylvester Stallone. His SEC is equipped with a supercharger, boosting the 5.6-litre V8 engine to some 320 bhp, enough for 165 mph (265 kph). Bulbous wheel arches cover massive tyres, a deep front air-dam balances the spoiler on the boot, and the interior is completely retrimmed in leather. This sort of attention from Koenig can easily double the cost of a big Mercedes.

Even the SEC conversion, however, is surpassed by another Koenig offering. They start with an already outrageously fast Ferrari Testarossa and turn it into a prodigiously turbocharged rocket-ship, which has Maranello fans grinding their teeth in anguish, but Koenig's customers rubbing their hands with delight. In its "basic" version, the

RIGHT: *BMW's luxurious 850i coupé, widened and dropped almost to ground level by Koenig. Impractical outside the race-track, but some clients will suffer for style.*

BELOW: *Mercedes designed their SL sports car to be handsome and Koenig make sure you can't miss it. With its low suspension, wide wheels, extended arches and a hefty tail spoiler, it's unmistakable.*

Koenig's twin turbochargers increase the output to around 750 bhp, while modified body panels and dramatic spoilers make sure that no one mistakes it for just an "ordinary" Testarossa. One of these also sits on Sylvester Stallone's driveway. For the truly courageous, the tuning company have yet another option: they fit even bigger turbos and an adjustable boost control in the cockpit. Around the large control knob are the figures that back up Koenig's claim that this is the most powerful car you can buy: the "low" end says 800 bhp – the other, 1000 bhp! To drive – or maybe it's fly – a Ferrari with double its original power it will cost almost double the original price tag. Including the base car, Koenig charge anything up to DM 850,000 for this machine.

Astonishingly, this is still not the fastest car in the Koenig stable. For this adventurous tuning and conversion company also has

BELOW: Race-track refugee: the Koenig C62 is a road-legal sports car, derived from the Le Mans-winning Porsche 962C, and capable of an awe-inspiring 235 mph (378 kph).

its own version of Porsche's 962 sports-racer – the C62. This monster looks almost identical to the Porsches that raced at Le Mans, except for the higher headlamps, which are raised to bring them to the legally required level. At a phenomenal top speed of 235 mph (378 kph), the C62 relies on ground effects to keep it in contact with the tarmac, and its flat-six, turbo-charged engine hurtles the car past 60 mph (97 kph) in 3.5 seconds. Lift the tiny door and the narrow seats are slotted into the broad chassis with barely enough elbow room, and a virtually bare fascia proudly displays a 400 kph speedometer. But book a taxi for the suitcases, because the only luggage the C62 is designed to carry is a couple of attaché cases, which slot into the wide sills under the door. Still, luggage or no luggage, few other cars have the same impact when drawing up in front of a hotel.

BELOW: *If you are bored with your Ferrari, take it to Koenig. They will turbo- or supercharge it, lower it, and alter the bodywork to make it unique.*

BOTTOM: *The C62's cockpit is as extraordinary as its outside. The car is such a tight fit that the driver cannot fit his legs under a normal round wheel, hence the cut-away.*

High Wycombe's Supercar –
Schuppan 962CR

Not immediately associated with the building of supercars, High Wycombe, near London, became in 1992 the home of an astonishing, road-legal, Group C sports-racing car, the Schuppan 962CR. Brainchild of Vern Schuppan, a Le Mans winner and sports car team director, the car takes its mechanical parts from the Porsche 962C, which dominated Group C sports car racing in the 1980s. The 3.4-litre, flat-six engine can be tuned "down" to 500 bhp or up to 600; Schuppan retained Porsche's five-speed racing gearbox which, unlike most competition 'boxes, already has synchromesh. A new all-composite chassis makes a few concessions to road use, such as more ground clearance and easier access, and the CR's Kevlar body is softer and more attractive than the race cars, with an integrated tail-wing, indicators, and somewhere to put the number-plate.

It remains, nevertheless, essentially a sports-racer in concept. Inside the bubble cabin, the driver and passenger rub elbows and it is all but impossible to see anything behind, but here, technology comes to the rescue. When reverse gear is selected, a video screen on the dash comes on, showing the rear view from a mini TV camera placed in the back light. Air-conditioning and Connolly leather improve the occupant's comfort, and perhaps help to take their mind off the price, – approximately $1350,000 (£750,000). Although just having the money may not be enough to own one, because ex-works Porsche driver Schuppan vets prospective buyers for their driving skills. Driving any 200 mph (322 kph) vehicle is a heavy responsibility, and in the hands of the inexperienced or the reckless, a car with the staggering responses of a race-bred engine, the girth of a truck, and poor rear visibility could all too easily become a dangerous liability.

BELOW: *Powered by Porsche and made in Britain: Schuppan's 962CR road-racer has a softer, more stylish body than the 962 from which it borrows its running gear.*

GT40s: Old and New

If you hanker after a Le Mans racer from another era, it is now possible to buy a new example of a 25-year old car. The mighty Ford empire finally achieved victory at the 24-hour race in 1966 with the GT40 MkII, a mid-engined machine with a 7-litre Ford block under its handsome fibreglass panelling. Its radical looks (the name comes from the fact that the car is only 40 in/101.6 cm high) and the unusual way the door is opened (it takes much of the roof with it), have always guaranteed it plenty of attention even in the paddock, and its victories at Le Mans and other circuits have made it an automotive legend.

Thanks to its sturdy construction and the availability of parts for its production-based engine, the majority of the 120 or so built have survived, and many are still raced today. The fact that with a de-tuned engine they can also make an exciting road car makes collectors doubly keen to acquire one. Original GT40s are, of course, rare and are not often seen in the "for sale" columns, but if you can't wait there is an alternative.

Safir Engineering in Surrey, England, still build GT40s. They are accurate replicas in design and construction, and are officially sanctioned as the MkV version, with the chassis numbers following on from the last MkIV model assembled in 1967. Redesigned by the original designer to use a fabricated instead of a pressed-steel chassis, they are otherwise identical to the early MkI GT40. They rely on double-wishbone suspension front and rear, with firm springs and dampers attuned for adhesion rather than comfort. Engine specification is to the customer's choice, but most buyers choose a 5.3-litre Ford V8, tuned to produced 400 bhp together with plenty of torque. In the 1960s Ford built a few road versions of the GT40, called the MkIII. These had an extended tail with a neat boot tucked inside. The new car, though, is meant to look like the racer, so out goes the convenience of a boot and the radiator is in the nose, which means there is no storage space at that end.

This is a car for day trips to the race circuit, but only to watch. The new cars, though technically the continuation of the production run, cannot be used for historic racing – they are for highway entertainment only. Yet they remain as spartan and cheerless inside as the racers, despite their $405,000 (£225,000) price before tax. True enthusiasts would undergo almost anything for the chance to live out their fantasies along the Mulsanne straight in June 1966.

ABOVE: *Unbelievable but it is street legal. Although it is a new car the Safir GT40 MkV is the authorized continuation of Ford's sensational 1960s supercar.*

BELOW: *True to the car's origins, Safir install a Mathwall-tuned Ford V8 with serpentine centre exhausts. The muscular 400 bhp and bulldozer torque are no problem for the 5.3-litre block.*

The AC Cobra

Another "born again" machine is the ferocious AC Cobra. A big-block Cobra is now considered the epitome of the 1960s sports car, but when it was announced in 1962 there were plenty of observers who sneered at it, claiming that it was just a mongrel. It was an Anglo-American project, which took the attractive AC Ace – a car built by a tiny UK company who were having engine supply problems – and dropped into it a snarling, 4.7-litre Ford V8. American race driver Carroll Shelby was behind the project, and his company turned the Cobra into a successful racer, especially the later, coil-sprung, 7-litre version, which won the World GT Championship in 1965. The Cobra, incidentally, briefly became notorious in Britain when AC tested their coupé-bodied race car at speeds of 180 mph (290 kph) on the M1 motorway. At that time (1964) there was no speed limit, so these early-morning trials were not actually illegal, but the resulting sensational newspaper headlines sparked off a campaign that ultimately led to the current 70 mph (113 kph) limit.

Many Cobras have been modified or converted over the years, but one of the genuine 427SC (Semi-Competition) cars is the one every one is after. This is the hottest one of all, with a few legal details added to make it roadable. The muscular machine with its ear-splitting V8 wail has become a legend on both sides of the Atlantic. Demand for the crude, noisy and uncomfortable, but shatteringly fast snake has overtaken the supply – production was cut off in 1968. One dealer turned down an offer of $720,000 (£400,000) for his own SC. So it has gone back into production. An English firm called AC Autokraft which is based at the old Brooklands race-track, bought the original jigs and formers, and they now construct the AC MkIV with the full authority of AC and Ford.

With an improved chassis and larger cockpit, the new car is faster and more comfortable. But it is still hand-built in small quantities, so although it is cheaper than an original Cobra in good condition, it's not cheap. Depending on whether you want the dearer lightweight version, you could pay up to $360,000 (£200,000). However, much of the glamour and kudos of driving a Cobra has been deflated by the huge number of fibreglass replicas, which have been built on simpler mechanicals. Unfortunately, some of these replicas are very convincing, and there is nothing worse than pulling up in an expensive, authentic Cobra only to be asked "Did you build it yourself?"!

BELOW: *Although the original Cobra was a fairly basic machine, today's MkIV can be specified with leather trim and luxurious Wilton carpeting.*

OPPOSITE: *Born again: brutal, loud and fast, the AC Cobra of the 1960s has reappeared, mildy refined, as the AC MkIV. It's still loud and fast, but not quite so brutal.*

Isdera

If the discomforts of a legendary but windowless sports car or period Le Mans racer do not appeal, and an Italian supercar seems just too exotic – or too vulgar – then perhaps an Isdera from Warmbronn in Germany is the answer. The Isdera is a rare, low and dramatic roadster with the inestimable advantage of Mercedes-Benz reliability. Isdera, under its founder and designer Eberhard Schulz, has formed an unusually close relationship with the Stuttgart company, to the extent of using Mercedes' wind-tunnel to finalize the sleek shapes of the cars, which are produced at the rate of about a dozen a year.

Under its exciting fibreglass skin, an Isdera is surprisingly simple. The fabricated square-tube steel chassis structure carries suspension and other mechanical parts from one of the Mercedes models. Controls, instruments and fittings also come from the same source, giving the finished car a quality feel. Leather trim and cruise control add to the luxury appeal, while air-conditioning is almost essential for a car with such large, flat windows – otherwise the resulting greenhouse effect would be stifling in summer. Access is through huge gull-wing doors, which swing up from the centre of the roof, certainly enhancing the car's effect when it pulls up in the street. On the roof is a rear-view periscope, replacing the normal door mirrors, which attracts more questions from curious youngsters than the rest of the car.

The fastest of the range is the larger V12 engine Commendator, which borrows the 6-litre V12 of the Mercedes-Benz 600SL sports car. Or a customer may specify the more restrained 5.6-litre 32-valve V8, giving a mere 330 bhp. Instead of the normal front location, however, Isdera turn it round and install it behind the two-seater cabin, driving the rear wheels through a special gearbox and differential. With this power on tap, the smaller V8 engine Imperator can

LEFT: *Stunning looks and quality mechanics make the Mercedes-based Isdera one of the more practical supercars. This Imperator packs a 32-valve Mercedes V8 with 180 mph (290 kph) potential.*

reach 184 mph (296 kph), yet it can still be serviced by any garage used to dealing with more ordinary machinery bearing the three-pointed star. Reliability and low running costs are a big plus point when the car costs $234,000 (£130,000)!

Even more exciting was the amphibious vehicle specially built for Baron Thyssen, one of Europe's richest men. The Baron became bored with having to park his car and climb into his speed-boat when he wanted to visit the island he owns in the middle of Lake Maggiore in Italy. So he ordered a four-wheel drive motor boat – or perhaps it could be called an aquatic estate-car – with which he could drive into the lake, cruise across the water and emerge in front of his villa with dry feet. The Thyssen Sea-Ranger was offered to the public with a vast price-tag, but was such a huge machine that it was impractical on the narrow roads around the Italian Lakes, and it did not become a commercial success.

These examples clearly show the extremes to which some people are prepared to go for individuality. Some projects are more tasteful than others; some are unsophisticated, while others are pushing the frontiers of body design. But if you simply want gull-wing doors on your Mercedes, one of today's coach builders will be happy to oblige . . .!

BELOW: *Isdera founder and designer Eberhard Schulz is privileged to have access to the Mercedes-Benz wind- tunnel to create and refine his sleek dramatic profiles.*

ABOVE: *For open-air excitement, Isdera offer the Spyder 036i. Within the composite shell the tubular steel chassis cradles a 3.6-litre straight-six engine.*

SBARRO EXOTICS

For those who want to own a car that guarantees attention, how about a gull-wing Mercedes? Not the 1950s classic, but a radically revised 560SEC Coupé, structurally reworked by Franco Sbarro in Switzerland. This wizard of the one-off will design and execute virtually any project, no matter how bizarre, for any client wealthy enough to foot the bill. Past exercises include road-going replicas of some of the great sports-racers of the 1960s, such as the GT40, Ferrari P3 and Lola T70, a tiny hatchback driven by 12 cylinders of Kawasaki power, and another "supermini" which packs a Ferrari V8. Other replicas, either one-off for individual clients or available in small quantities, have covered the BMW 328 (the pre-war sports car, using a modern BMW 6-cylinder engine), a Mercedes 300SL, and a copy of Mercedes' handsome and rare 540K roadster of 1936. Sbarro has even built a replica of the fabled Bugatti

Royale, a vast construction driven by two Rover V8 engines linked to make a 7-litre V16!

Sbarro also create machines that are more than just replicas. In response to the four-wheel drive movement, Sbarro and his engineers created a huge off-roader, which used a 6.9-litre Mercedes V8 and sat on enormous wheels taken from a Boeing Jumbo Jet. With eight chromed exhaust pipes emerging through the bonnet, this device was appropriately named "Monster". When a Middle Eastern ruler wanted a desert car to hunt from, Sbarro complied with a six-wheeled shooting-brake called Windhound. This mighty machine on its fat, all-terrain tyres has a central throne in the rear compartment and an electric roof. When the scouts sight suitable game, hydraulic pistons elevate the VIP's seat through the roof to give him an ideal field of fire — in maximum luxury.

LEFT: *Franco Sbarro has been behind some of the most outrageous automotive creations ever. The wedge-* *shaped Challenge has a turbocharged Mercedes V8, four-wheel drive and a rear-view TV camera.*

BELOW: *The wheels of Sbarro's "Monster" off-roader come from a Jumbo jet. This company is never short of ideas to indulge the fantasies of the wealthy and extrovert client.*

The end of an era: the Rolls-Royce Phantom VI is the last limousine to be hand-built on a separate chassis. This landaulette (open at the rear) was built for a Middle Eastern head of state.

PHANTOM VI

THE PHANTOM

A fitting close to this chapter is the very last hand-built limousine to emerge from the workshops of Mulliner Park Ward, the coach-building arm of Rolls-Royce Motors. Since 1927, Rolls-Royce has had a Phantom model as the flagship of its range, the basis of the grandest and most luxurious limousines. In 1991 the very last example of the series, a Phantom VI, was completed, ending for ever a chapter of motoring history. This was the last coach-built car with a separate chassis to carry the famous Flying Lady mascot.

The Phantom VI is the model often used by Her Majesty the Queen and many other heads of state on formal occasions, but the last, and 365th, P VI was ordered by a private English client. Taking over 20 months to build, the 20ft-long machine weighs three tons, but it can easily surpass 110 mph (177 kph) with its 6.75-litre V8 engine. The alloy body is assembled, by hand, from many separate panels, painstakingly shaped and repeatedly checked against the massive wooden body buck – it can take three weeks to perfect the form of just one of the wings.

In the rear compartment, tradition reigns. There is no television and no fax machine, though there are two telephones. Instead, the passengers relax on velvet upholstery, screened by silk curtains, the expanse of walnut veneer is relieved by a solid-silver fruit bowl and flower vases. Inside the inlaid cocktail cabinet are goblets made of silver, with magnets concealed in their bases to keep them steady on the folding tables. Ice is kept in the fridge in the boot. There is also a barometer, an altimeter – and an electric pencil sharpener. The total cost is naturally a confidential matter between the customer and Rolls-Royce, but the final price for a "basic" Phantom VI was quoted as $630,000 (£350,000); this example will have cost considerably more.

There will never be another limousine built in this way, clothing a separate chassis with coachwork involving this degree of care, skill and tradition. The delivery of the car to the owner's fleet (which includes another Phantom, an ordinary Rolls saloon, and a Bentley Turbo R) marks the very end of a glorious era.

In a field bristling with new technology and rapidly changing styling, "this year's model" has been the focus of car-buyers' aspirations since the first Motor Shows – and those were before the twentieth century began. Only in the last 20 years or so has a new phenomenon arisen – the vintage car as art. Instead of being sought-after only by old-car buffs, or providing cheap racing for those who could not afford an up-to-date racing car, older cars, led by the best Ferraris and Alfa Romeos, began to rise in value noticeably faster than other collectable items. Faster, for a while, than virtually any other financial investment it was possible to make.

Like the top end of the art market, the finest vintage cars are all catalogued and known about. If you have a desire to own a vintage Bentley or Bugatti, you can go to a specialist dealer who will either have one or two in stock, or know of an owner who might be persuaded to sell. But if your collection is missing an example of the very best, the rarest, most prestigious, then you must be patient. For instance, only 50 supercharged Bentleys were built, Bugatti supplied around 30 Type 57SC chassis, and the 2900B Alfa Romeos numbered fewer than 40. Such cars rarely go publicly up for sale. To own a car like this you must know where the car is and who actually owns it, for many are bought by agents or holding companies.

It is an odd contradiction that although owning and driving a handsome vintage car is a fashionable and enjoyable self-indulgence, some collectors find good reasons to keep quiet about the extent of their collection. In the interests of security, for example; an efficient team with a truck and trailer could easily make off with several million pounds-worth of motor car, and with less risk involved compared to robbing a bank. Often the taxman might be all too interested in the overall value. And in the USA, where alimony is big business, more than one enthusiast keeps his hoard in two groups: the one the wife and her lawyers know about, and the one they don't.

There are four factors that make a vintage car desirable. Its rarity, its inherent engineering quality, the beauty of its bodywork, and its recorded history. Inevitably this tends to focus interest on sporting machinery, particularly with a racing history. Given that outright racing cars have a limited use, it is the fastest sports cars which are at the top of the list. Alfa Romeo and Bugatti were ardent rivals and prolific winners in the 1930s, both on track and road. These dual-purpose machines remain extremely sought-after for their high-quality manufacture, elegant lines and very high performance.

BELOW: *The perfect blend of beauty and function: Jano's wonderful 8C 2300 Alfa Romeo brought repeated race wins to the Milanese marque. This is one of the short-chassis cars raced by the legendary driving ace Tazio Nuvolari under team manager Enzo Ferrari, and it carries his prancing horse shield on the scuttle.*

RIGHT: *The symbol of a very special car: the cavallino rampante ("prancing horse") and the letters SF for Scuderia Ferrari, the works team which Enzo Ferrari ran before he built his own cars.*

Alfa Romeo

Central to the mystique of Alfa Romeo is the name of Vittorio Jano, one of the greatest automotive designers, who joined the company full-time in 1926. While earlier Alfas had begun a tradition of race successes, it was Jano's designs that carried the Milan company to its greatest heights. Alfas of this period were high-quality, expensive machines of six or eight cylinders, designed specifically to win races. This was a time of open road racing, and the most famous of these races was the Mille Miglia – 1,000 miles (1,609 km) of non-stop punishment over a route which combined miles of flat-out straight with tortuous, unfenced, mountain passes. With the exception of 1931, Alfa Romeo won it every year from 1928 to 1938.

Of the cars used it is the supercharged 8C cars that have the edge for enthusiasts today. Four consecutive wins at Le Mans from 1931 to 1934 and a string of other victories in sports and racing form pushed Alfa on to an unprecedented plane of success – despite their financial problems. This success was achieved before the engine was developed into the power-unit of one of the greatest single-seater Grand Prix cars of all time, the Tipo B, or P3. As it first appeared, Jano's famous eight had a capacity of 2.3 litres and an unusual layout. To avoid the flexion problems of long crankshafts, he split the engine into two blocks of four cylinders. Helical gearing at the centre of the crank drove the twin overhead camshafts, the water and oil pumps, and the supercharger. Even in standard form the power output was 130 bhp, and competition examples rose to 180 bhp. Under the bonnet, the engine itself is a beautiful sight: heavily finned manifolds of silken alloy, solid castings designed apparently without thought of cost, and the general appearance of being built to win.

The semi-elliptic sprung chassis came in two lengths, the longer known as the Le Mans, since they ran there with four-seater bodies. Short-chassis, or Mille Miglia, cars are lighter and more manoeuvrable, and often carry gorgeous two-seater bodywork by Touring or Zagato. This car is one of the true high points of automotive history: beautiful, lovingly assembled, agile and very fast. Speeds of at least 105 mph (167 kph) were normal, and tuned examples reached 130mph (209 kph). Most people are astonished to learn that an 8C with the larger 2.6 capacity will easily out-accelerate a modern hatchback GTi to 60 or 70 mph (97 or 113 kph). No wonder that one of these changed hands at Monaco in 1989 for $3.2 (£1.76) million. It is, of course, relatively easy to cut down the long chassis from a saloon or coupé 2.3 and turn it into an MM, thereby boosting its value. Buyers, therefore, need to do careful research to ensure that the car they are buying is what it claims to be.

It is also possible to convert a 2.3 into the Monza spec, and the result is still a wonderful car – as long as the converter is honest about what he has done. But certain chassis are particularly special; if proof exists that this is a works car with a famous driver or a great victory behind it, the car becomes priceless. Before founding his own car company, Enzo Ferrari ran the Alfa works racing team under the Scuderia Ferrari banner. On the scuttle, his cars bore the yellow shield with the prancing horse. Many vintage Alfas have had this painted on, but those which are entitled to it are very desirable indeed.

OPPOSITE: The unmistakable radiator grille, bearing the famous roundel and evocative script, identify this as one of the great cars of its period – indeed of all time.

BELOW: Factory race cars could produce as much as 180 bhp from the supercharged twin-cam 8, a work of art in itself. This gives the 8C a performance that could embarrass some of today's machinery.

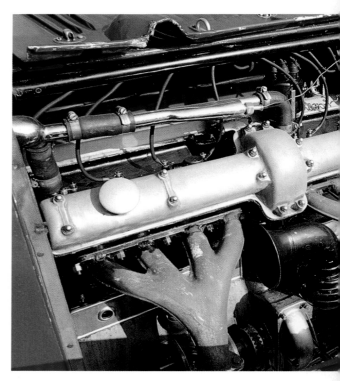

THE MONZA

In 1931, Grand Prix rules still required two-seater body-work, and Alfa built an even shorter version of the 2.3 to compete. Differing from sports versions by having an external exhaust, a pointed tail and a cowled radiator, the new car won its first Grand Prix, the Italian GP at Monza. Since that win the model has been known as the Monza. Today, in 2.3 or bored out 2.6 size, it is one of the most usable cars you could own for racing or touring. Fitted with mudguards it is capable of a Continental foray (admittedly with minimal luggage!) or a quick trip to Silverstone. At the track you can enter it in a vintage sports car race and expect to win if the driver is up to it, while minus its mudguards and headlights it qualifies as a Grand Prix car – and is likely to be competitive in that field too! A Monza is one of the highlights of the spectacular collection assembled by American fashion magnate Ralph Lauren, who displays selected cars every year at the most glittering *concours d'élégance*, such as Pebble Beach. A real all-rounder, even rarer than a Zagato 2.3, any Monza is a million-dollar machine.

BELOW:
In two-seater Grand Prix form the 8C became the Monza when it won its debut race, the Italian GP. This handsome dual-purpose machine is greatly prized today.

The 2900B

History was reversed when the Tipo B racing car, whose engine had been derived from the 8C 2.3, came to the end of its competitive Grand Prix life in 1936. Despite the heroic efforts of Tazio Nuvolari, one of the greatest racing drivers of all time, the Alfa could no longer beat the Silver Arrows – the all-conquering Mercedes and Auto-Union teams from Germany. Sensibly, the factory decided to switch its efforts back to sports car races. Its stock of Tipo B engines, in enlarged 2.9-litre twin-supercharger form, provided an ideal power source, and the factory drew up a sophisticated new chassis to utilize it.

Called the 8C 2900B, the new car boasted all-independent suspension, using twin trailing arms at the front and swing-axles with a transverse leaf spring in the tail. A four-speed gearbox in unit with

BELOW: In the face of the all-conquering German steamroller in Grands Prix, Alfa Romeo switched its efforts to sports car racing, resulting in the sensational and advanced 2900B.

the differential gave it excellent balance, especially in the shorter of its two wheelbases. With 180 torquey bhp and many lightweight aluminium components, the 2900B was a revelation in 1937. Its acceleration was astonishing, particularly at higher speeds where unblown cars would be running out of breath, and the supple suspension gave it remarkable road-holding. Speeds varied from 120 mph (193 kph) up to 140 mph (225 kph) for the special light examples, which scooped the first three places in the gruelling Mille Miglia in 1938.

These advanced and expensive cars – the bare chassis price was £2,035 – were clothed in simple and elegant bodies by Touring of Milan, in both spider or coupé form. The lucky owner of a long-chassis coupé could enjoy a mix of comfort and performance, which was almost unequalled by any other pre-war car, and arguably not matched until the 1950s. Fewer than 40 2900Bs rolled out of the factory, which makes them amongst the rarest and most sought-after of all classic cars, and explains the £1m recently paid for a *coupé lungo*.

Even now, to drive a 2.9 is an electrifying experience. Press the tiny throttle pedal – situated between the clutch and brake like many vintage cars – and the car surges ahead with superchargers whining and exhaust crackling. Its steering is alive and responsive, the ride well controlled, and the handling balance a delight. It is still a high-performance car by today's standards, and quite remarkable for a pre-war machine.

BELOW: *Twin camshafts, twin superchargers and upwards of 180 bhp: the beautifully built powerhouse of the 2900B gave it electrifying performance which was years ahead of its time.*

LEFT: *Most of the 30 or so 2900s received perfectly proportioned bodywork from Touring of Milan. This is one of the beautiful short-chassis spyders, with plunging grille and sculpted running boards.*

Bugatti's Type 57

One of the few possible rivals to the 2.9 Alfa came from the Bugatti plant at Molsheim in France. A glittering racing record, exquisite engineering, and a dedication to sheer style made the Bugatti name a glamorous one, and the Type 57 is one of the greatest creations of a single-minded man. Ettore Bugatti, like Enzo Ferrari after him, preferred to perfect a design rather than experiment with too many new ideas, but even if he appeared to be slow to follow the technical advances of others, the cars he designed were of such beautiful craftsmanship that they rank as mobile art.

First seen in 1933, the Type 57 had a 3257 cc straight-eight, twin-cam engine, and was offered with a range of dramatic coach-work designed by Ettore's son Jean. Despite its conventional leaf-spring layout, the chassis proved to have fine handling, which was further improved in the 1936 sports version, the 57S. Originally the 57 could not quite reach 100 mph (161 kph), so the factory offered a supercharger and called it the 57C, for Compresseur. But the *crème-de-la-crème* of the range is a sports chassis with the supercharged engine – the 57SC, capable of over 130 mph (209 kph). A mere 30 were built, making it rank with the Alfa 2900B in performance and in rarity, though some 40 or so S models were supercharged later.

BELOW: *Every Bugatti excites collectors, but the Type 57 is very special and the 57SC (sports chassis with supercharger) is the most desirable of these. This example has a coupé body by London coach-builder Corsica.*

BUGATTI "ATLANTIC"

Europe's most flamboyant coach-builders loved to dress Bugatti chassis, and the Type 57 received some outrageous and some very beautiful bodies. Their appeal varies, though all are valuable, but if forced to pick one model of Type 57 many connoisseurs would select an SC with Jean Bugatti's amazing "Atlantic" coupé body. It is sensuously streamlined, featuring unique external riveted flanges on the roof and wings. This, too, figures in Ralph Lauren's impressive stable. It is a dream to drive, but only in cool weather because it has no ventilation and the heat from the underfloor exhaust makes it stifling. Three Atlantics were built, and though they have only changed hands privately, rumours suggest that the most recent buyer paid more than seven million dollars.

Ettore Bugatti's son Jean, later tragically killed driving one of his father's cars in 1939, displayed his inventive design skills with the amazing Atlantic coupé on the 57SC chassis.

The Royale

Yet there is another Bugatti which is even rarer, more fabled, and – hard to believe – even more valuable – the Royale. This was Bugatti's "Car of Kings", intended to appeal to the crowned heads of Europe – though none actually bought one. In fact, Bugatti only ever sold three Royales, while the family retained another three for their own use. It was the most expensive car ever sold. When new the chassis price was over $7,200 (£4,000), a staggering sum in 1931. Fifty-six years later, one of the six, with a body by French coach-builder Kellner, went for auction at Christies in London. The hammer fell on a bid of $9.9 (£5.5) million, an all-time record for an automobile which stood for three years.

All six Royales still exist, each with a unique body style. It is an enormous car; the eight-cylinder, single-cam engine displaces no less than 12.7 litres, and the cast aluminium wheels would carry a truck.

BELOW: *The car built for kings – but their majesties declined to buy. Ettore Bugatti retained this Royale for his own use. Today it is one of the stars of the astonishing Schlumpf museum in France.*

LEFT: *Bugatti intended the Royale to be the best car in the world. It was certainly the costliest, being listed in 1931 at £4,000. In 1986 this one, the Kellner coach, raised £5.5 million.*

LEFT: *Jean Bugatti designed this vast two-seater for a M. Esders. The original body was removed and replaced; this replica was built at the Schlumpf museum on a spare chassis frame.*

Yet only one of the cars produced looked like a limousine. On a car that was already so extreme, the few *carrossiers* who had the opportunity (including Jean and Ettore Bugatti) produced bodies ranging from a sort of 19th-century carriage to what must be the biggest two-seater car ever made. Its owner, a French industrialist, commanded Jean Bugatti to design it without headlamps, as he did not intend to drive it after dark.

Bugatti had hoped that the Type 41 Royale would secure him the position of the builder of the greatest car in the world, eclipsing Rolls-Royce, Hispano-Suiza and Isotta-Fraschini. Commercially it was a memorable failure, arriving on the market at a time of depression. Cynics have claimed that the radiator mascot, an elephant standing on its hind legs, was a tacit admission that the car was a white elephant. Historically, however, it has guaranteed Ettore Bugatti exactly the aura he always craved – for being creator of the biggest and costliest car in the world.

BELOW: *Symbol of pride or a wry joke? The Royale's radiator mascot of an acrobatic elephant was created by Ettore's sculptor son Rembrandt.*

W.O. Bentleys

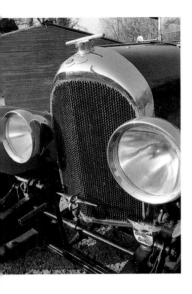

ABOVE AND BELOW: *The Bentley legend began with the 3-litre. There were only four cylinders, but it had the sophistication of four valves per cylinder. Quality engineering means that many are still running and racing today.*

In contrast, and often in competition with Molsheim, the Bentley marque substituted mass for finesse, and torque for high revs. Tall, solid, heavy and durable, Bentleys epitomized the British sports car of the late 1920s. These qualities meant that the cars were especially suited to the punishment that a 24-hour race exacts, and they proved this at Le Mans. Their victory in 1924 was an early signal for the then unheard-of string of four wins from 1927 to 1930.

Road-racing success was not, unfortunately, enough to keep the company solvent. Despite substantial private backing by one of the team's best drivers, millionaire Woolf Barnato, Bentley failed in 1931 and was bought by Rolls-Royce. Unable to build any more cars under his own name, W. O. Bentley himself moved to the Lagonda company. Rolls-Royce has continued to build fine cars with this famous

badge, but for vintage enthusiasts, a "real" Bentley is one designed pre-1931 by the man whose name appears on it. These are known as "W. O." or Cricklewood cars after the location of the factory, and it is amongst these that the finest and most desirable examples are found.

Thanks to their tough construction, a great many W. O. Bentleys have survived until today. However, their very reliability and sturdiness has meant that keen owners have never stopped using them. Inevitably, thanks to wear and repair, engine swaps and body modifications, there is barely an unmodified car left, and of all things, originality is paramount to a collector. Of course, keeping a car in regular use is the best thing for it, and very laudable. But the type of use has naturally changed, and many Bentleys originally carried saloon bodies for everyday usage. Today using such a car tends to be a special occasion, and very many saloons have been turned into open tourers.

Of all the Bentleys, the prime specimens are naturally the team cars, those that carried the Union Jack to victory at Le Mans and elsewhere, driven by the wealthy, glamorous crew known as "the Bentley Boys". Whether four-cylinder, in 3- and 4½-litre form, or the 180 horsepower Speed Six of 6½-litres, which triumphed in 1929 and 1930, the sale of one of these cars would have buyers bidding from all over the world.

BELOW: *Today everyone wants a Le Mans Bentley. This style of coachwork is the most rakish and the most desirable especially for use in events such as the Mille Miglia.*

The Blower Bentleys

In 1930, in an effort to keep his Bentleys ahead of the opposition, Sir Henry Birkin, the marque's most dashing champion, commissioned engineer Amherst Villiers to supercharge the 4½-litre engine. W. O. disliked the idea, but Birkin and the racing "Blowers" brought a final flush of fame to the winged "B", pitting the massive British touring cars against the cream of Continental racing machinery. Birkin's most memorable feat with a Blower was to come second to a GP Delage in the Grand Prix of Pau in 1930, and the very Bentley he manhandled over this tight street circuit is another gem now found in the Lauren collection.

Apart from Birkin's five team cars, a limited run of 50 Blowers was built, and their rarity and performance make them especially valuable today. They are not easy cars to drive. One has to admire the stamina of Birkin and Barnato and the others who wrestled with the heavy steering, stubborn crash gearbox and jarring ride for long hours in endurance races. Over the years, many owners of blown and unblown cars have succumbed to the temptation to rebuild their cars into Le Mans specification: fabric replica Van den Plas body, huge fuel tank on the tail and wire stone-guards on the lamps. Although such conversions used to be frowned on in vintage circles, this style of car is what many collectors want and prices have soared. A good one can easily command $900,000 (£500,000). Nothing, however, can equal the prestige of one of the handful of remaining "proper" team cars (two of which have belonged to the same collector for many years), and if one came up for sale, the sky would be the limit.

ABOVE: *Designed by Ferdinand Porsche, the huge Mercedes S had its supercharger controlled by the throttle pedal. A firm push cut in the blower for straight-line power.*

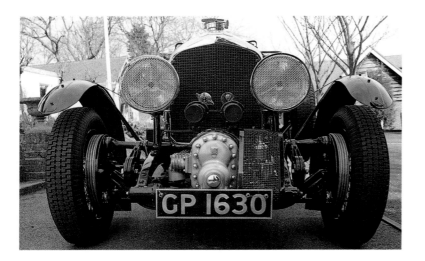

LEFT: *Despite W. O. Bentley's opposition to the idea, and their relative lack of racing success, the Blower 4½ has become, arguably, the most glamorous Bentley of all.*

The S and SS
Mercedes-Benz

Blower Bentleys have superchargers that run constantly. Mercedes-Benz chose a different approach for its equally massive S and SS sports cars in the 1920s. The huge six-cylinder engine normally ran unblown, but with an extra shove on the throttle pedal, the driver could cut in the supercharger for straight-line sprints. Hearing one of these great cars leaping forward from a bend, as the ear-piercing shriek of the blower comes on, is one of the electrifying moments of vintage racing.

Designed by Ferdinand Porsche, the S appeared in 1927 with a 6.8-litre, overhead cam engine and the blower standing vertically at the front of the block. Soon afterwards the more powerful SS took the power up to 200 hp from 7.1 litres. In the hands of Rudi Caracciola and his team-mates, the white cars wailed to victory in sports car

BELOW: *In a shortened, more powerful form, Mercedes boasted 225 bhp from the SSK, of which they built only around 30.*

ABOVE: *Because of the immense value of these cars it is very rare to see one in action on public roads. This example was snapped on the 1988 Mille Miglia retro-run.*

races and hill-climbs all over Europe, roundly beating the Bentleys in the 1929 Tourist Trophy in Ireland. By 1931, and driving a faster, shorter variant, Caracciola was unbeatable.

Built as prestige "flag-wavers" for the company, all these cars are rare – there were fewer than 300 S and SS models assembled. Usually seen with low, tourer bodywork, their immense size and chromed triple exhaust pipes poking through the bonnet strike awe into bystanders. But what makes the enthusiast's heart beat wildly today is the sight (or sound) or the short-chassis SSK. With the pedal down and the enlarged blower engaged, an SSK pumped out 225 horsepower through its skinny tyres, enough to carry it to 140 mph (225 kph) and beyond. Production figures only ran to the low thirties, putting this fearsome machine firmly into the very top rank of collectable motors.

Mercedes-Benz did build an even faster version, a works race-entry known as the SSKL (L for leicht, or light). A big blower, drilled chassis and 300 horsepower made this the ultimate development of the S series. Only a handful were built, but unscrupulous dealers are thought to have converted other models to this specification more recently. Since historians disagree over numbers, the sad result is that experts view any car claiming to be an SSKL with suspicion. An SSKL with a proven history, though, must be regarded as a Holy Grail of classic cars – rarer than rubies and priced above platinum, the sort of car that simply does not come on to the open market.

540K MERCEDES

Slightly less rare is the 540K Mercedes, a 5.4-litre sports-tourer, which arrived in 1936. It had all-independent suspension, a supercharged, eight-cylinder engine, producing 180 bhp and a speed of well over 100 mph (161 kph). Again it is highly sought-after, this time for its comfort and elegance rather than for a racing pedigree. The "best" 540K is often considered to be the Special Roadster, a rakish factory two-seater with flowing chrome-edged wings and tail. A derelict, but complete example found in a barn in England was snapped up at auction in 1988 for £1.6m – before restoration costs!

ABOVE: *The pinnacle of Mercedes grand touring luxury cars before the war was their 540K, a super-charged, all-independent cruiser which easily tops 100 mph (161 kph). Bodywork could be by Mercedes or specialist coach-builders.*

The Duesenberg Model J

European manufacturers prided themselves on offering the finest automobiles, but it took an American marque to scoop up some of the royal custom Ettore Bugatti wanted. With the engineering skill of Fred Duesenberg and the entrepreneurial flair of E. L. Cord, the Duesenberg company in 1928 launched its Model J, now a byword for quality in automobile manufacture. Its 6.9-litre, eight-cylinder, twin-camshaft Lycoming engine boasted four valves per cylinder, and an output of 265 bhp, streets ahead of its rivals. In fact, the J instantly eclipsed anything else on the American market: it was faster (116 mph/187 kph), more sophisticated, longer, lower, and very, very expensive. By 1933 the factory was listing one model at the unbelievable price of $20,000, a sum that would still buy a good car today.

Like many top-rank machines, the Model J came as a bare chassis to be clothed individually to the purchaser's taste, either by the factory or one of the best coach-builders. The famous and the wealthy vied with one another to own more and more elegant examples: Hollywood stars, industrialists, princes and Maharajas bought Duesenbergs – and flaunted them. With its exquisite craftsmanship and lavish instrumentation, the Model J demanded the chance to show its pace in action.

In 1932, a supercharged model appeared – the SJ – capable of 129 mph (207 kph) and with an increase of power to 320 bhp, and its shorter chassis endowed it with even better handling. These are the most coveted Duesenbergs. Of the fewer than 500 Model Js produced, only 36 were SJ versions, including two very special extra-short wheelbase cars – one each for Gary Cooper and Clark Gable. With such a rarified pedigree, no wonder that one of these changed hands for $2.07m (£1.15m).

There are, of course, many other deeply desirable pre-war cars apart from those mentioned here. In an era when the rich owner could commission the most lavish and beautiful coachwork on the finest chassis, there are wonderful examples of Hispano-Suiza, Rolls-Royce, and Isotta-Fraschini. Rakish Delahayes, luxurious Cadillacs and the advanced Cord from the USA all deserve to be used and maintained by enthusiast owners. But around certain machines a mystique grows up, and when such mystique combines with restricted numbers and innate engineering quality, a car can become a mechanical legend.

ABOVE: *The Model J saved Duesenberg from obscurity, though not from collapse. Fast, silent and built to exceptional standards of quality, owning a J is a life-long ambition for many car lovers, but an impossible dream for most. This is a 1931 Murphy aluminium top coupé.*

For many people, the cars they desire most are those of their youth, when their enthusiasm matured before their driving licence. Today's successful and wealthy man may well be looking back nostalgically to the 1950s or 1960s, to the sports cars he coveted when reading about Le Mans, the Nurburgring and Watkins Glen. And with the widespread new interest in classic cars, there is a plethora of outings to show them off. These retrospective runs have intensified from the light-hearted day trip to the three tough days of the Mille Miglia around Italy and the gruelling Carrera PanAmericana, which is a whole week's racing across the width of Mexico.

Theoretically, these are not true races, only rallies with time targets. But the targets are often so hard to attain that the cars end up careering over mountain roads at breakneck speeds, urged on by enthusiastic onlookers. Entry is exclusive; it's essential to be rich (the entry fee alone for the Mille Miglia is over $5400/£3000) and it helps to be famous. Film stars mix with famous racing drivers and even royalty. The Brescia square, which forms the base for the Mille Miglia, brings together Phil Hill, Stirling Moss, Riccardo Patrese, and Prince Michael of Kent – a keen car lover often seen in such events driving Lagondas and Aston Martins. Even being rich enough to afford an appropriate

BELOW: *For three days in May the Italian town of Brescia revolves around the Mille Miglia retro event. Rows of priceless Alfas, Ferraris, Bugattis and Maseratis queue in the main square, making this the greatest moving car museum in the world.*

OPPOSITE, BELOW: *A giant step – in 1952 Mercedes created the wonderful gull-wing 300SL. It achieved victories at Le Mans and in the Carrera, and almost won the Mille Miglia in an astonishing début year. Road cars followed two years later.*

car does not guarantee entry to this over-subscribed event. The famous may be invited to crew someone else's machine, and receive the adulation of the crowds who line almost every mile of the route.

Even tougher and more dangerous, the Carrera PanAmericana recalls the short-lived, but legendary, road-race across the American continent in the early 1950s. In those days the rules were few and the dangers great, as cut-down Chrysler and Chevrolet saloons mixed it on dust roads with factory racers from Mercedes and Lancia. Today's re-creation of that event reflects the risks. The regulations do not demand genuine period cars, and many people enter replicas of famous sports cars. Here you may see Mark Knopfler taking time out from writing and performing with Dire Straits to accompany London socialite and race driver Alain de Cadenet on a week of hardship, dramatic scenery – and risk. Steve O'Rourke and Dave Gilmour of rock group Pink Floyd had a narrow escape when their replica Jaguar C-Type went off the road in Mexico and was virtually destroyed in the 1991 event.

Today these events are purely for kicks for lucky owners, but the originals were serious undertakings aimed at grabbing headlines. Mercedes-Benz sensibly chose the competition route to rebuild its prestige after the devastation of World War II, and in just a few years swept first the sports car and then the Formula One arenas. Its sports contender was the famous 300SL, another technical leap which caught rivals napping.

BELOW: *Facing the dangers of the 1991 Carrera PanAmericana are (from left) Steve O'Rourke, GP driver Guy Edwards, Dave Gilmour and Alain de Cadenet. Celebrities O'Rourke, and Gilmour (of Pink Floyd), crashed next day, as did de Cadenet.*

105 HYY

Mercedes 300SL

Starting with a solid, but unpromising six-cylinder motor from the weighty 300 saloon, the Stuttgart engineers created a tubular steel space-frame with alloy panelling, which was light and strong and very clean aerodynamically. To maximize the strength, the sills were very high, and instead of normal access there were the famous "gull-wing" doors, which make the model so memorable. Thanks to meticulous engineering and preparation, Mercedes almost won the 1952 Mille Miglia, and went on to victories at Le Mans and in the Carrera in Mexico. It was an astounding début year, and it had customers clamouring to buy this sensational sports car.

Mercedes obliged in 1954 with an improved 300SL road car, sporting fuel injection and some of the showroom comforts its wealthy buyers wanted, but retaining the unique and stylish upward-hinging doors. Capable of 150 mph (241 kph), it was the fastest car in production at the time, and it quickly became a favourite road car for star race drivers. A convertible followed in 1957 with improved rear suspension, which diminished some of the more treacherous aspects of the swing-axle system. This is arguably a better road car – though purists claim it is merely a soft *boulevardier* – but its conventional doors lack the novelty of the coupé. 1,858 roadsters were made, but the bidding goes much higher for one of the 1,400 Gull-Wings – today one could reach perhaps $450,000 (£250,000).

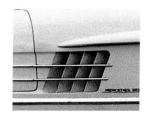

BELOW: *For the American market, Stuttgart developed a convertible. Although in some ways a better car it has always remained less collectable than the famous gull-wing.*

The Jaguar Racers

In the 1950s manufacturers invested time, money and effort, not to mention the safety of their star drivers, in the great races in order to promote sales of their more conventional products. It is debatable whether Jaguar's Le Mans successes of the 1980s affected the values of the marque's earlier great cars. It was in any case a time of soaring prices, so thoroughbreds, such as the Le Mans-winning C-type and D-type, were bound to increase in value as fast as any other collectable car. This might have brought wry smiles to the faces of Jaguar executives in the 1950s, when the company was forced by race homologation rules to build more race cars than it wanted, and was then unable to sell them.

There was, however, no problem in selling the mainstream Jaguars. The Coventry company's almost unmatched blend of comfort, speed and sheer good value made the XK120 sports car, introduced in 1948, a huge success. Over 10,000 were built. After a standard car performed well at Le Mans in 1950, Sir William Lyons, the father of Jaguar, ordered up a lightweight race version. This became the C-type. Under its lovely alloy skin, a tubular steel chassis carried an XK engine tuned up to 200 bhp. Wide-based wishbones at the front and a trailing-arm, live rear axle gave it fine handling. It won the 24-hour race on its first time out in 1951. Two years later Jaguar added the new Dunlop disc brakes and outran everyone else for a second victory.

C-types were built for sale to privateers, too, and by the time it was replaced by a new competition car there were 53 of them. Naturally, not all of these have survived, making original examples few and far between. Thanks to the long-lived XK engine, which only went out of production in 1990, owners have been able to go on enjoying their C-types in historic racing and on the road in the burgeoning retrospective events, such as the Mille Miglia re-runs. Rarer than the more famous D-type, though not quite as covetable, it is a car to admire and to have fun in, hence its auction record of £878,000.

ABOVE: *C-types are scarcer than the more collectable D, but they are a thrill to drive and an ideal entry for one of the road-race retro events.*

The D-Type

1954 saw the début of the D, even more specialized, even more gorgeous to look at. It featured a monocoque centre section with a subframe carrying the engine and front wishbone suspension. Trailing arms attached to the rear bulkhead located the rear axle, and naturally there were disc brakes all round. Revisions to the XK engine, including fitting three twin-choke Weber carburetters, produced 250 bhp, which could push the low-drag shape right up to 200 mph (322 kph) for the three daunting miles of the Mulsanne straight. Although Jaguar only managed second place at Le Mans that year, the following year in 1955 saw the first of a trio of wins, which endowed the D-type with the lasting glamour of victory.

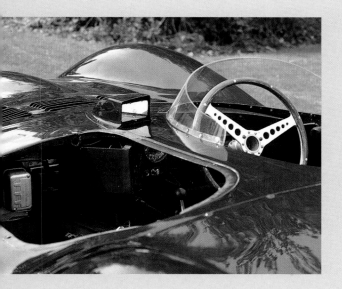

Some old racing cars have only reappeared with the recent growth of historic racing. But a D-type is a very usable car, with a torquey and willing motor, and they have in the main been carefully looked after and properly exercised. Out on the road, the spine-tingling wail from the straight-six engine and the snarl from the enormous Webers makes driving one a thrill to boast about for weeks afterwards. On open road, classic car events, such as the Mille Miglia, a Jaguar is one of the best cars to be in. It is fast, exciting and more reliable than a highly-strung, supercharged, pre-war machine. Enthusiastic Italian onlookers go wild as the green cars scream past and chant "Jag-war!", with almost as much fervour as they shout "Alfa!". That makes it very desirable, but they don't come up for sale very often, and when they do they fetch staggering prices – the auction record is £1.21m.

The XKSS

Race regulations should have compelled Jaguar to manufacture at least 100 D-types. In the event, they only built 87, and many of those sat around in the factory gathering dust. The idea of this makes today's classic car lovers weep, but at the time not many people wanted to buy a spartan competition car. So Jaguar decided to make the D more appealing by adding touring equipment. The result was the XKSS: basically the same running gear and body, but with a curvaceous, chrome-framed windscreen and a skimpy hood. Instead of the D's two separate cockpits, the centre bar was removed, making the car look more conventional. Inside, some leather trim and a speedometer were deemed enough to turn it into a tourer, though the only luggage capacity was a chromed grid on the tail.

Race enthusiasts view the XKSS with disdain, seeing it as a soft version of a D. But in 1957, after only 16 XKSSs had been completed, fire destroyed the factory. No more D-type or SS models were built, hence that figure of 87, which makes the road version even rarer than the race car. Now if you wanted to own one of the race winners you would have to be prepared to go to the owner with a blank cheque. However, as often happens, a car's provenance has some hiccups. The 1955 winner, for example, was later cannibalized to rebuild another car, but the remains were rebuilt as well – so which one is the "right" car? A famous owner can also inflate interest in a particular car, balancing up a lack of race history. Hence the crowds drawn to the Lynx engineering stand at Earls Court Motorfair in 1987 by the XKSS on display, a favourite toy of film actor Steve McQueen.

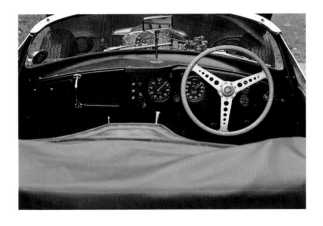

ABOVE: *Removing the centre bar makes the XK-SS slightly roomier; a speedometer, missing from the race versions, reinforces the road-legal character.*

BELOW: *In an effort to sell its unwanted Ds, Jaguar added a windscreen and hood to produce the XK-SS. Some, were factory conversions of basic D-types with just enough equipment to make it a rapid tourer.*

Ferrari's 250GTO

One of Jaguar's main opponents at Le Mans in the 1950s went on to become probably the most evocative name in motoring – Ferrari. The company's history is one long parade of speed, beauty and racing success. From the collector's point of view there is barely an undesirable Ferrari in the entire output of the Modena factory – even the most common models (the pretty Dino and the 308/328 range) are wonderful cars. If you draw up outside a restaurant in anything with a prancing horse badge you are guaranteed to cause a stir.

Nevertheless, every crown has its jewel, and amongst Ferraris this must be the 250GTO. This is the archetypal road-race car, built in 1962 to whip everyone else on the track in the GT category. Noisy, fast and beautiful, it was the most talked about Ferrari for many years – until the arrival of the F40. In its time it typified Ferrari's outrageous flouting of the rules. It had the bare minimum of interior equipment to count as a grand tourer rather than a racing car, but it completely failed to qualify in terms of numbers. International regulations demanded that at least 100 examples be built to qualify as a production car, in order to prevent companies from building a few outright racing cars to clean up in the touring class. But Enzo Ferrari was a realist. He knew that he couldn't sell 100 frighteningly fast and desperately ex-

BELOW: *Fast, loud and beautiful – the most coveted Ferrari of all. The dual-purpose 250 GTO is at home on the track or the road, and can scream up to 175 mph (282 kph).*

pensive cars. He was also by then so sure of his importance to the racing world that he was quite open about the facts. He had plans to build around 39 cars and he was stopping at that. It was enough; the authorities allowed the car to be homologated, and the letter "O" for "omologato" was added to the name.

Developed from the successful 250 series, which began in the 1950s, the GTO was the ultimate embodiment of the front-engined road and competition Ferrari. It was an evolution rather than a technical advance, combining the basic layout of the previous 250 SWB (short-wheelbase) car with the power unit of the legendary Testarossa sports-racer. Three 4-litre cars were built, but the rest have a 3-litre V12, crowned with a colonnade of polished intake trumpets for the six twin-choke Webers. This endows it with 280 bhp, enough to propel the low, curvaceous body, with its unmistakeable trio of air inlets across the nose, up to 175 mph (282 kph).

Despite its simple technology, using a live rear axle and leaf springs, the GTO's handling is excellent, even if the ride is jarring. Aerodynamic details like the wing slots show that it means business, and the sensational noise is enough to give goose-pimples to any car-

BELOW: *Three scalloped air-intakes are one of the GTO trademarks, though these handbuilt cars vary in detail. This is one of only three 4- litre cars, which are more flexible and relaxing than the 3-litres.*

lover lucky enough to be overtaken by one. It is neither the most successful nor the rarest Ferrari, but most people see it as the greatest of a great line. That is why in 1990 at Monaco, a GTO sold for the highest price any car has ever achieved – a staggering £6,350,000 ($11,430,000). And that is without auction premiums! That, of course, was at the height of the classic car market, and only one year later, when another GTO came up, the bidding closed at a disappointing £3.2 ($5.76) million. It is a lucky man who, like pop promoter Pete Waterman of Stock, Aitken and Waterman fame, can walk into his garage and admire the scarlet lines of his own GTO.

The 250 Testarossa

If victory on the track is the primary criterion, rather than the dual-purpose appeal of the GTO, then an older Ferrari springs into focus – the 250 Testarossa. First cousin to the 250 grand tourers, it first appeared in 1957 and by the following year it had matured into a world-beater. Testarossas brought Ferrari the World Sports Car Championship in 1958, 1960 and 1961, including two wins at Le Mans, the most prestigious arena of all.

But victory laurels are only part of the Testarossa's appeal. The sensational looks of the early examples are unique. A tear-drop bonnet scoop hides the twelve carburettor chokes of the 3-litre engine, and ties in visually with the slender wings that stand proud of the body. This "pontoon" style was intended to maximize airflow to the brake drums (Ferrari was still resisting using discs), with large cutaways behind the front wheels to remove the air. In practice the aerodynamics proved rather inefficient, and later cars had conventional bluff fronts and smooth sides.

The 250 is no tourer, as inside the shallow cockpit there is nothing but bare aluminium. A slender wood rim makes the wheel warm to hold, if the ferocious heat coming from the engine isn't enough, while the blast over the low perspex screen will batter anyone but a midget. Despite the current popularity of vintage racing, few would dare race a TR, so it is only on retro-runs, such as the Great American Race and Ecurie Ecosse Tour in Scotland, that you are likely to see one outside a museum. Naturally there is no protection against the weather, so if it pours during the run the crew had better have their oilskins handy. Mind you, there's no boot either . . .

Much of the Testarossa's success was achieved by the works team, which included stars like Mike Hawthorn, Phil Hill, and Peter Collins. But TRs were built for sale to private teams too, even if they were usually one step behind the factory's latest development. Although these cars were the sharp end of sports car racing – state-of-the-art racing machinery – the final production total of 33 almost matches the number of GTOs, also supposedly a production car. This is still a very rare car, the sort that the dedicated collector stalks for years before the right opportunity comes up. So far most exchanges have been private, but there is no doubt that seven figures are always involved.

BELOW: *Its cutaway "pontoon" wings were designed to help cool the Testarossa's brakes. They didn't work very well, but these cars are still more desirable than later conventional shapes.*

LEFT: *The all-conquering Testarossa brought Ferrari the sports car World Championship in 1958, 1960 and 1961. It's a racing car through and through, with no crew comforts.*

Aston Martin's GTs

Although the GTO is still top of the price chart, the expanding popularity and number of retro-events on public roads has pushed road-racers, once valued but not very practical, right up alongside the tourers and luxury vehicles, which used to command the most attention and the highest prices. During the steep increase in values of the late 1980s, it was the Aston Martin marque that shot up fastest, quickly joining Ferraris and pre-war Alfa-Romeos as the superstars of the most glittering and theatrical auctions.

First to peak were the road-racers again, Ferrari's track rivals of the 1960s becoming their auction rivals 20 years later. The Zagato-bodied lightweight DB4GT, first seen in 1960, represents the culmination of Aston Martin's efforts in the GT class. It is stunning to look at, muscular

LEFT: *Zagato used a similar body-style on several other chassis, notably Fiat and Bristol, but its simple lines looked absolutely perfect on the Aston.*

and compact, and possibly the single greatest design to emerge from the idiosyncratic house of Zagato. There are 19, all surviving and well documented, plus the four "Sanction 2" cars described in Chapter 3. They vary slightly, as handmade cars will, but the most perfect in line and history are still known by their registration numbers "VEV 1" and "VEV 2".

These two were made famous by Jim Clark, Roy Salvadori and Innes Ireland. In fact, the Zagatos just couldn't match the Ferrari 250GTs, and were eclipsed when the GTO arrived, but that does not deflect Aston enthusiasts. A DB4GT Zagato is the one they would sell their grandmothers for, and when both VEV 1 and VEV 2 came up for sale at separate auctions, collectors began to drool at the idea of a matched pair. However, with a final combined price of almost $5.4 (£3) million, the idea was too much for any single buyer and the two famous machines went to different homes.

LEFT: *Some race drivers claimed that the Zagato was no better than the plain GT, slightly lighter, but less predictable. That doesn't put enthusiasts off!*

The Ford GT40

In an earlier chapter we met the GT40, the Le Mans winner that brought so much prestige to the Ford name in the second half of the 1960s. These cars were built to race, and there is barely one that does not have competition history, even if it is a "road" version which has only recently started vintage racing. In various guises, from small-block 4.7 to 7-litre MkII, the GT40 was a competitive car for six years of racing. Its illustrious career was dramatically rounded off in 1969 by just about the most exciting Le Mans win ever. After 24 hours hard duelling, Jacky Ickx beat the Porsche 908 of Hans Herrmann by a mere hundred yards. The car he drove had also been the winning machine the year before – the first car ever to win the endurance classic twice. That car has to be the most desirable GT40 of all. Yet each one of the 120 or so examples that remain has a story to tell. Several were used as camera cars for the two greatest racing films ever, *Grand Prix* with James Garner and *Le Mans* starring Steve McQueen. Both actors subsequently became enthusiastic drivers themselves, but were banned by their studios from competing in top-level racing, turning instead to the less risky area of off-road racing.

Oddly enough, the road-going version of the GT40, which Ford marketed briefly in 1967, is rarer than the competition one. Called the MkIII, it should not be confused with "road" versions of the MkI and MkII, which merely had some token additions such as reversing lights and a Ford badge, but otherwise looked similar. Using the same chassis, MkIII cars had higher front wings to bring the headlamps up to a legal level, and a long tail containing a slender luggage boot. There was softer springing to preserve the owner's insides, and a new central gear-change to allow left-hand drive; like most sports-racers, GT40s were right-hand drive with a right-hand gear-change, making an LHD version impossible. It was an expensive cul-de-sac for Ford, as only seven MkIIIs were assembled. One was bought and used by Herbert von Karajan, the Austrian conductor – a point of interest in its favour – but in general they are not as highly regarded as the others.

RIGHT: *Just 40 inches high – hence its name – Ford's GT40 was a tough and reliable race car with a second life as an exciting but gruelling road car.*

ABOVE: *Thwarted in its attempt to buy Ferrari as a flagship, Ford went one better and put its own name to a car which, in one form or another, won at Le Mans three times – the GT40.*

Of course, it is a rare occasion when one of these cars can properly show its paces. At ordinary speeds it is simply strolling, but to open it up requires long, empty roads. Most of the time driving it is something of a trial, as there is little ventilation, room for either a spare tyre or luggage, but not both, the visibility and the lock are both bad, and it needs acres of parking space, because those doors with their roof cut-outs have to be fully open to let the inhabitants scramble out. If it is only attention that you want, every trip is a kick, but if you want to explore the car's exceptional performance you will need to head for the widest open spaces you can find.

The Bentley Continentals

A racing background is not essential to make collectors drool over a car. There are one or two post-war Bentleys that reach peak prices, although the company's racing years were long past by then. Designed to blend high speed with long-legged luxury, the Continental models broke away from being merely re-badged Rolls-Royces and displayed their own sleek and streamlined shapes. The earliest and most striking are the R-type Continentals, with a lowered radiator shell (though still commanding by today's standards), a sweeping wingline and fast-back, two-door styling, which brought the speed up to 120 mph (193 kph).

Subsequent Continentals became faster and increasingly comfortable, gaining power steering and air-conditioning, and eventually in 1960 a 6.2-litre V8 engine to replace the old inline six. But it is the simpler, lighter and more elegant R-types, with their aluminium bodies built by H. J. Mulliner, which are the epitome of the Continental Bentley – and which will drain the budget most. A fine example is as dear as a new Ferrari 512TR, though quite a contrast in style. Yet this must be one of the most usable of classic cars. It is silent to ride in, with a commanding view over lesser traffic, as well as having a performance that will surprise many modern cars. Inevitably, as with all the best things, they are few and far between. Fewer than 200 rolled out of the Mulliner works, and those lucky enough to have one guard them jealously.

RIGHT: *In the 1950s, Bentley offered the wealthy customer 120 mph (193 kph) luxury for four people. But post-war Britain could not afford the R-type Continental, the most expensive car in the world, and they went for export only.*

The Lamborghini Miura

Also without a competition history, but at the opposite extreme to the Bentley, is Lamborghini's first "great", the Miura. Its unveiling at the Geneva show of 1966 amazed everyone – customers, the press and rival manufacturers. It was mid-engined when only racing cars were; it had a transverse V12 engine layout, which remains unique even today; and its stunning Bertone-designed body boasted lines of a simple beauty that have rarely been rivalled. With a 4-litre engine, taken from the more conventional front-engined tourers that preceded it, the Miura could touch 180 mph (290 kph). Although the few people who tried to reach that speed found that it was not to be recommended, because flawed aerodynamics tended to lift the front wheels right off the ground at 170 mph (274 kph) or more.

For everyday use though, the Miura is a dream. Its design, by the engineer Dallara, used a strong, steel centre monocoque to cradle

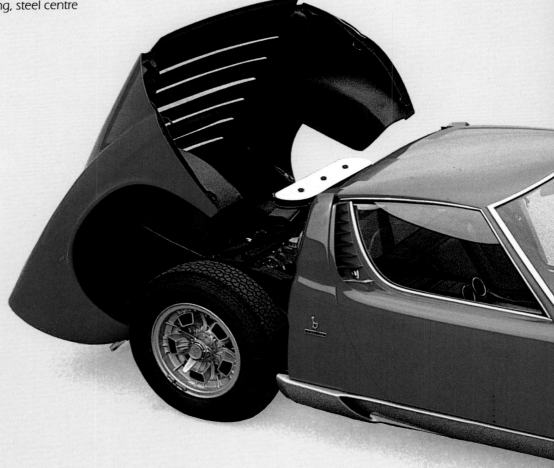

LEFT: *Arguably one of the most beautiful shapes ever put on the road, Bertone's body for the Lamborghini Miura clothes an innovative and clever chassis.*

the engine and its integral transmission, with the suspension affixed to this structure so that the nose and tail panels were unstressed and could be removed for repair or maintenance. There is a proper spare wheel in the front, half-hidden by the windscreen, and a small boot squeezed into the tail, making weekend trips a possibility. In the small cabin, the driver lies back with legs stretched, and ahead the taut curves of the front arches are nearly invisible, hidden by the drilled steering wheel and the twin cowls of the rev-counter and speedo-meter. Despite the hand-stitched leather, this is not a luxury machine. The two rows of dials and the alloy, open-gate gearshift all point to performance above comfort, and the snorting carburettors and whir-ring cam-chains ram the point home as the revs rise.

This heady blend of speed and beauty culminates in the Miura SV, of which only 170 (out of a total of 760 Miuras) escaped the Sant'Agata works before production finally switched to the Countach in 1973. Engine modifications brought the horsepower up to 385, and

LEFT: *Under the tilting tail, the Miura's unique transverse V12 engine layout is obvious. Suspension loads feed into the monocoque, leaving the "clam-shell" body sections unstressed.*

suspension changes put more rubber on the road, which gave the SV impressive road-holding and a little bit more performance than the original P400 and S models. That is why the Lamborghini enthusiast desperate to capture one needs to have at least $180,000 (£100,000) in his pocket before ringing round the dealers.

Whether it was the international oil crisis of 1973, or the threat of legislation which looked as if it might kill or at least hobble the sports car, the 1970s were in some ways a rather barren time for prime, sporting machines. The new generation of 1970s road cars, like the Countach and the Ferrari Boxer, were better propositions than ever. But sports car racing technology had moved on so far that these vehicles were quite unable to attain glory on the track, and in any case were being mass-produced with no real variation. The rally circus, however, did throw up some interesting novelties. These are the "homologation specials", cars produced in the minimum number required to compete in rallying and dedicated only to winning.

These forerunners to the Porsche 959 and Ferrari F40, like Jaguar's unsellable D-types, often lingered around the factories and the showrooms, too noisy, cramped and highly strung to find buyers. Today, though, rarity is everything, and prices of, for example, Lancia's Stratos have soared. To win the International Rally Championship three times, Lancia's competition department used up some 40 Stratoses in the mid-1970s. But to homologate it, the firm had in 1973 to build 400 of these stubby mid-engined machines, which are powered by the Ferrari Dino V6 engine and use fibreglass bodywork on a steel monocoque. Buyers for the twitchy, hard-riding machine were hard to find, and the model was still listed in the catalogue as late as 1981. In fact, Lancia gave some away as presents to high-selling dealers. The unlucky ones managed to sell them – the lucky ones pushed them into a back shop and forgot about them. Today those give-aways are worth sums approaching $180,000 (£100,000).

ABOVE: *The Miura was the first mainstream mid-engined sports car, and it was a revelation for 1966. Ferrari stuck to a front-engined layout until 1973.*

LANCIA STRATOS

Lancia's competition image in the early seventies depended on rally successes. As its Fulvia model became outclassed, the company realized it had no new car powerful enough to compete. The rules demanded that at least 500 examples be built; this was specifically to deter manufacturers from building hot specials, but Lancia bit the bullet and took the bold step of designing an all-new car just to win the World Rally Championship.

Lancia having been taken over by Fiat, Team Director Cesare Fiorio was able to select the powerful 2.4-litre V6 engine from the Ferrari Dino, also part of the Fiat empire. He chose a mid-engined layout for traction, and installed it in a steel monocoque built by Bertone. The fibreglass body was the most startling rally car ever unveiled, and enthusiasts cheered as it snarled its way to World Championships in 1974, 1975 and 1976.

The Stratos was not the first "homologation special", but it was the most extravagant. Lancia needed perhaps 40 cars for its entire rally programme; the rest of the 500 were just expensive surplus ironware. Some sources claim they built only 250, but either way many Stratoses lay unsold in showrooms across Europe for years.

Today this "sleeper", with its Ferrari engine, sensational looks and remarkable practicality, is beginning to catch up with other great classics as a collector's choice, helped by replica makers who offer otherwise unobtainable spare parts. It was just too early: if built today, buyers would flock to Lancia showrooms.

ABOVE: *Paul Newman's interest in cars began with the 1969 film* Winning. *Since then the film star has won national sports car championships, driven at Le Mans, and become a successful team-manager and mentor of new talent.*

PREVIOUS PAGE: *Neil Corner at Silverstone in 1991, proving that even the world's most valuable racing car is meant to be used. Behind his Mercedes W163 is World Champion John Surtees in the D-type Auto-Union.*

LEFT: *Fans agree that Le Mans is probably the best movie ever made on motor racing. Star Steve McQueen did his own driving, though his plan to contest and be filmed in the real 1971 race was thwarted by worried film producers.*

Motor racing has always been as glamorous as it has been expensive. From the era of the wealthy amateurs between the wars, who were able to race because they were rich, to today's millionaire stars who are rich because they race, top-level motor racing has continued to burn up money. Of course, there have always been the paid professionals: Tazio Nuvolari, Rudi Carracciola and René Dreyfus all earned fees as well as laurels. But in the 1920s and 1930s an enthusiast with enough funds could buy a competitive Grand Prix car, such as a Bugatti or an Alfa Romeo, and expect to get an entry in one of the major events. He might even beat the factory cars, though they usually benefited from certain mechanical tweaks that private owners did not get.

In the 1960s the wealthy amateur could still buy a car and crew and run at the back of the Formula One pack. Within a decade, however, the drivers were all professional and the teams heavily sponsored. One or two private backers did appear, such as Canadian millionaire Walter Wolf, who ran his own team (his cars sported the same black and gold livery as the Lamborghini Countach he used on the road), and the sporting peer Lord Hesketh. There have been notable amateur sports car drivers, though, and amongst them are two of the biggest stars on film.

Most car lovers will have seen the film *Le Mans*. Possibly the best motor-racing movie yet made, it portrays the late Steve McQueen driving in the famous 24-hour race, and much of the footage is genuine race action. By the time the film went into production McQueen was a proficient sports car driver with several victories under his belt, and he planned to race in the Le Mans event as it was being filmed in 1971. But the film company got cold feet, and his participation was limited to a later session when they hired the track for more filming.

Paul Newman has had a more satisfying experience since being fired with race enthusiasm after making a film called *Winning* in 1969. He went on to notch up a series of championships in American sports car racing, and in 1979 competed at Le Mans in a Porsche 935. Today his Newman-Haas Racing Team is one of the dominant forces in the field, and Newman has proved as good a team manager as he is a driver.

Today the amateurs have gone from the big events. Beer, tobacco and television sponsorship have inflated the costs to staggering levels. Formula One teams build their own cars and pay their drivers retainers of several million pounds. The friendly paddock atmosphere of the 1960s is long gone, replaced by wire fencing to keep the onlookers well away, motor-homes with blacked out windows for the stars to retire to, and helicopters and private jets to whisk them away. There is no place here for the amateur. Yet, with the sole exception of Le Mans, there is precious little style attached to any other division of modern racing below Formula One. It is many years since smart society flocked to motor racing as it once did at Brooklands. Today, the already rich and glamorous who want to be involved have turned to another area of the sport: old cars.

We have already considered the popularity and cost of sports-racers, which have a double life, being suitable for both circuit racing and road use. Whether for high-intensity transport, in retrospective classic car tours, or at *concours d'élégance* events. Racing cars, however, are an altogether more committed area, since these machines can only be used on the track, and only when there is the right sort of race for them.

BELOW: *While media pressure in Formula One has become so intense that today's heros jump straight from car to motorhome, protected by tinted glass and wire fences, vintage racing is becoming the fashionable place to be seen.*

Vintage Sports Car Racing

For years, an obsolete racing car was merely a curio, worth little, and with nowhere to drive it. Many were scrapped, some went into museums, while others received the care of a small band of private owners who admired their history and engineering. In Britain there have been regular vintage races since the 1930s, when the eligible cars were four or five, or at the most 30 years old. The club behind these, the Vintage Sports Car Club, was set up in 1931 by car lovers who felt even then, 60 years ago, that the golden age of sports and racing cars was already past.

The movement that they spearheaded and maintained, despite being viewed as thoroughly eccentric for many years, is now the fastest-growing area of motor sport. There are races for every type of car from the pre-World War I era to the 1970s, Grand Prix cars to family saloons. Crowds at these high-profile events now rival and even surpass mainstream racing; the timetable is full, and the grids are packed.

117

So is the paddock, because being just a spectator isn't enough – you have to be wearing a team pass to be chic. Racing old cars has become a highly fashionable pastime, instead of an eccentricity.

An even more marked development is the arrival of sponsorship. Where vintage racing once meant family picnics in the paddock, there is now likely to be a VIP tent, team uniforms, and even advertising stickers on cars that have never before carried anything but their maker's name. There are still picnickers, but now they bring hampers with gourmet spreads. Hermes scarves and Ray Ban sunglasses adorn the figures in the pit-lane, and autograph hunters are on the prowl.

Although the presentation has changed the racing has not. Vintage motorsport has thrived for years, and there are some excellent drivers involved. It is also considerably more spectacular than much of modern racing. The sight of Bugattis, Bentleys, and Frazer-Nashes sliding sideways through a corner on their narrow tyres, drivers working wildly at the wheel, brings cheers from the crowds. Amongst race machinery, the same names stand out as amongst sports cars: Alfa Romeo, Ferrari, Bugatti, Maserati. The cream of vintage engineering with the history to justify their place on the winners' rostrum. But there are fresh names to be added, too; single seaters from ERA, Miller, Auto-Union, BRM and Vanwall.

There are races for Edwardian cars, and the sight of a towering Itala thundering into a hairpin alongside a 60 hp Mercedes is one of the great events in racing. Few people realize that a Mercedes like this, introduced in 1903, has staggering acceleration and despite possessing the aerodynamics of a barn, can top 100 mph (161 kph). At these speeds, the driver, exposed from the knees up, is clutching the wheel to avoid being simply pulled off the huge machine by the blast, while only inches below his elbows the massive chains which turn the rear axle are thrashing round unprotected.

To propel this fearsome device there is an enormous 9.2-litre four cylinder engine. That means that each cylinder displaces more than today's average saloon engine! Its modern layout was a technological leap for the period, comparable to the impact of the Porsche 959 70 years later, and in the same way rich sportsmen clamoured to buy one, though the chassis alone cost $3,240 (£1,800). And many owners ordered two bodies, one closed for winter and an open tourer, which would be swapped over when the season changed.

Few remain, and historians have not been able to identify if any of those is one of the factory's successful racers. Even in the

INSET: Slow-revving Edwardian engines had to be large to provide the power. The 60 enclosed almost ten litres in its massive cylinders cast in pairs.

OPPOSITE: The Porsche 959 of its day; Mercedes crystallized racing car design in 1903 with their 60 hp machine, and the later 70 hp shown here. It was fabulously expensive then and it is amazingly fast even today.

pioneering days of 1903 the company appears to have painted up several cars to resemble the winner of the important Gordon Bennett Trophy, and displayed them simultaneously at Mercedes showrooms around Europe. Nevertheless, the performance and historical importance meant that one example achieved an auction record for a veteran car of $2.7 (£1.5) million.

Bugatti's Vintage Racers

As soon as we enter the inter-war period, Ettore Bugatti's name springs up. His steady engineering progression crystallized in 1924 with the Type 35, one of the all-time highs of automotive excellence and beauty. The elegant horseshoe radiator and slender pointed tail of these stark but handsome machines amassed a wealth of race victories around Europe, and made stylish road-cars for his rich and fashionable clients. Today owning any Type 35, or one of the similar-looking variants, is a source of great satisfaction. When these machines were designed, racing cars carried a riding mechanic and needed a second seat. Thus the T35 is a Grand Prix car that can compete in sports car races and be driven on the road.

BELOW: *Ettore Bugatti saw beauty as integral to fine engineering. Today, his Type 35 remains one of the greatest designs ever – perfect lines in a supremely successful package.*

Bugatti was careful to reinforce his racing effort by selling the same cars to private owners, and at different times offered eight and four-cylinder, single or twin cam, unblown and supercharged variants within the same body profile. Top of the Bugattiste's shopping list must be a 35B, its 2.3-litre, supercharged, straight-eight offering 130 bhp and a delicious exhaust sound – until you have heard it you can't appreciate why it is often likened to the sound of tearing cloth.

But as always a good pedigree can double the value, and this is particularly true of GP Bugattis. With their hard racing careers, often unbroken since the 1920s, there has been much repairing, re-placing and improving. When the spares ran out, people began to make them, and today it is possible to build an entire Grand Prix Bugatti from scratch. Worse still is the temptation to dismantle a gen-uine car, separate the pieces into two piles, and build both up into complete vehicles. Which, if either, is genuine? Cynics say that there are more GP Bugs around than the 660 or so which came out of the Molsheim factory. For this reason, a known history, or provenance, is immensely important. It can mean the difference between $270,000 (£150,000) for a clean straight T35 and $900,000 (£500,000) for a famous one, like the Type 51 (the twin-cam version), which was delivered new to J-P Wimille the French race ace.

And the Bugatti racing canon rounds off with what many claim is the most beautiful racing car ever designed – the Type 59 of 1933. Plainly derived from the well-known T35 shape, it is lower and sleeker, and distinguished by its unique radial-spoked wheels. Twist-ing forces were taken by the huge brake-drums, whose toothed edges lock directly into the wheelrim.

Despite a 3.3-litre straight-eight engine, the T59 did not have the success of its forebears. Today only some eight exist, and Neil Corner is one of very few owners bold enough to race one. If it weren't for enthusiasts like this, we would be able only to gaze at this beautiful machine, instead of seeing and hearing it doing the job it was built to do – to race.

ABOVE: *Even a Bugatti engine is a handsome artefact. This supercharged straight-eight unit provides the power under the bonnet of a 35C.*

LEFT: *While the Bugatti Type 35 is pretty, the later Type 59 is sensational.*

ABOVE: *Bugatti's trademark is the evocative horseshoe radiator, here gracing a 1926 35T. The shape and the oval red badge have identified virtually every Bugatti built.*

RIGHT: *Obsession: in the 1950s and 1960s the Schlumpf brothers secretly amassed a staggering collection of Bugattis in their factory in Mulhouse, France. Today it is a public museum.*

Alfa Romeo's Tipo B

We have already mentioned the Alfa Romeo Monza, the Milan company's rival to the Type 35 Bugatti; the two cars still meet and do battle in vintage racing. But if the 1920s was Bugatti's decade, the 1930s belonged to Alfa and the Tipo B. This clean-lined machine is a single-seater, complying with the new GP rules for 1932, and in its day it swept the Grand Prix field until the might of Germany took over with Mercedes and Auto-Union. Alfa sold them to private owners as well as running its own team, under Enzo Ferrari, and built around 12. The whereabouts of only some 8 are known, and if they change hands at all it tends to be secretly. At their Monaco sale in 1989, Christies knocked one down at a new record for a Grand Prix car – £1,960,000. Several P3s, as the Tipo B is often known, are high and dry in museums, though you can see one or two racing at the most important vintage meetings like the Pittsburgh Grand Prix in the USA, the Oldtimer GP at Germany's Nurburgring, or the Christies' Historic Festival at Silverstone, England.

BELOW: *Speed, beauty and an exceptional pedigree: Alfa Romeo's twin-supercharged Tipo B was sensationally successful in its day, and the few that remain make a stirring sight and sound on the track.*

Collectors and Collections

At these major gatherings the paddock is a fashion parade. Elegant women step around mechanics lying on their backs under cars, film stars and musicians mingle in the VIP suites, and bottles of fine wine are liberally distributed. Even the car parks are packed with exotica – there is nowhere better to turn up in your prized Lamborghini, Bentley or Ferrari than a motor-race, where the bystanders will appreciate it. Amongst the top rank of historic racing, some owners hand their cars over to experienced drivers, who are well used to the oddities of racing old cars on their skinny tyres.

One exception is Nick Mason. Stalwart drummer for superstar rock band Pink Floyd, which is merely a sideline to his real passion of motor racing. A keen enthusiast from his youth, his musical success has allowed him to assemble one of the finest collections of racing cars anywhere. Often seen at the wheel, racing his Type 35 Bugatti or his Maserati "Birdcage" sports car, Mason himself is an accomplished and dedicated driver, who turns out to chilly November club events as keenly as the big meetings. He has raced at Le Mans in a Porsche 956, but is more often found dicing amongst the historic Grand Prix cars in his beloved Maserati 250F.

Last of a proud line of single-seaters, Maserati's 250F has a wonderful-sounding, straight-six engine inside a simple and beautiful body. It is for many people the most attractive front-engined GP car of all. First built in 1954, it was a top GP contender for several years, winning the World Championship in 1957 for the legendary Argentinian driver Fangio. With its torquey 2½-litre power-plant and a transverse gearbox in unit with the differential, the 250F is a delight to race. The sight of Nick Mason or Willie Green swapping places with the Ferrari Dino of Neil Corner is one of the best you can see anywhere.

ABOVE: *An aficionado through and through: Nick Mason, drummer for rock group Pink Floyd, races his fine cars whenever he can – and frequently wins.*

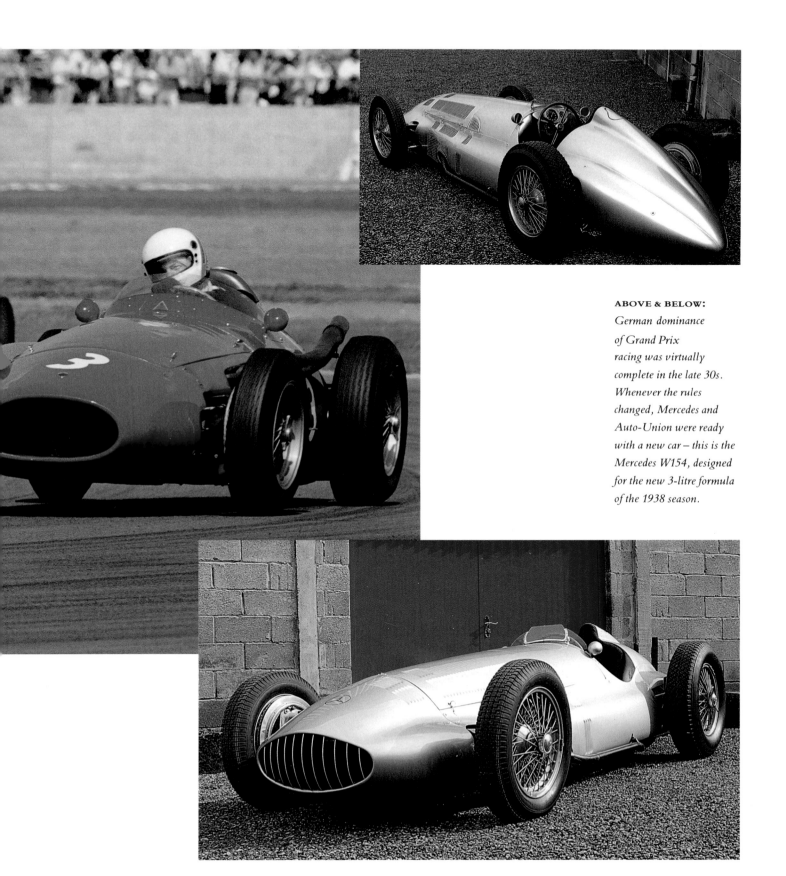

ABOVE & BELOW:
*German dominance
of Grand Prix
racing was virtually
complete in the late 30s.
Whenever the rules
changed, Mercedes and
Auto-Union were ready
with a new car – this is the
Mercedes W154, designed
for the new 3-litre formula
of the 1938 season.*

Naturally, all vintage racers would love one of these great and beautiful cars, but their values vary widely – from expensive to frightening. Maserati built around 30 cars, depending how strict you are on the very confused histories of many of them. And in recent years an English enthusiast has built eight new ones using some factory parts. He was careful to mark them as new cars, but inevitably one or two are now in other countries posing as originals. However, an authentic example, with the right documents and photographs, could be worth a million pounds – so temptation is understandable.

Another devotee is Neil Corner, who has amassed and races an impressive stable, which includes two fabulous giants: one of the few Mercedes Grand Prix cars still running and a V12 Auto-Union. These two reflect the pre-war days when the Silver Arrows from Germany steamrollered everyone else on to the sidelines, and since both makes are as rare as hen's teeth, such a pairing in private hands is quite an achievement. Corner proved his dedication to racing when in 1991 he actually raced his priceless Mercedes in a GP event, the Christies Historic Festival at Silverstone.

Corner's is not the only Auto-Union running in Britain. Tom Wheatcroft, the building magnate who has rescued Donington Park circuit in Derbyshire from dereliction, boasts a V12 in his stunning museum, the Donington Collection, where 130 racing-cars are on show. This is one of the greatest assemblies of single-seaters anywhere in the world. On a quiet day, Wheatcroft rolls one of the gleaming machines across the road and on to his own circuit, so that the Derbyshire hillsides can relive the days before the War when the Silver Arrows came to Britain – and conquered.

Amongst the cars that occasionally appear and give demonstrations on the track are the only running survivors of some of the most fabled machinery ever. In Nick Mason's collection is the rare BRM V16, the over-complex and unsuccessful attempt to put Britain at the top of the Grand Prix league. The car was never sorted out in the 1950s; its memorable legacy is not its victories, but the extraordinary howl it makes on full song. Mason's car is one of two running examples (Tom Wheatcroft has the other), and those lucky enough to hear them on one of their rare demonstration outings can be grateful that their owners are true enthusiasts who like to exercise their cars.

Donington Park is a working race circuit, where vintage and classic races take their turn with formula racing, trucks and motorbikes. But Wheatcroft is not the only collector who has a track where he can

BELOW: When the Silver Arrows came to Britain before World War II they raced at Donington. Today the track is home to Tom Wheatcroft's amazing collection of single-seaters, including this V12 mid-engined Auto-Union.

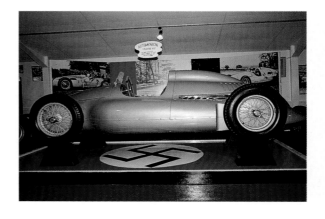

exercise his racing cars. In the south of France lives one of the great Ferrari enthusiasts, Pierre Bardinon. Despite the often-repeated dictum that Ferrari never sells its obsolete racing cars, he has assembled an outstanding display of road, sports and single-seater Ferraris. To keep them fresh – as sitting still is bad for a car – he can start one up and take it out on to the private track he has built around a small lake on his estate.

Further north, outside Paris, a pair of tall stone gates leads down a long tree-lined avenue towards a moated chateau. Alongside, a stone barn conceals another collection containing cars from France, Britain, Germany and Italy; sports cars on one floor, Grand Prix cars above. An electric hoist can pick up any one of these well-maintained machines and deposit it on the apron outside, for nearby, in a wooded meadow, is a small and beautifully smooth race track. There are no facilities for the public, this is purely for the pleasure of its owner. It has to be heaven on earth for the passionate motor-racing lover.

BELOW: *James Garner is another Hollywood star hooked on cars and racing. His film,* Grand Prix, *with its innovative multi-screen images, is one of the most dramatic racing movies ever made.*

INDEX

PICTURE CREDITS

All pictures supplied by Mirco De Cet except for the following: p9 Andrew Morland; p76, 83b LAT magazine; p82, 88–89, 91, 100–1, 112–13, 114b, 116, 124 Chris Harvey.

Quintet Publishing would like to extend special thanks to the following for their help in supplying pictures:
Autocraft Ltd., Weybridge, England; Bugatti Automobili SpA, Modena, Italy; Cizetta Automobili Srl, Modena, Italy; Koenig Specials GmbH, Munich, Germany; Isdera GmbH, Leonberg, Germany; Musee National de l'Automobile, Collection Schlumpf, Mulhouse, France; Sbarro Ltd, Les Tuileres, Switzerland;
Paul Faulkes Halbard at the Filching Manor Motor Museum, Polegate, Sussex, England for supplying the Bugatti type 35, Bentley 3 litre and the 1931 Alfa 8C 2300;
Neil Corner Collection for supplying the 1938 Mercedes racer, Bugatti type 49 and the Ferrari single seater Dino.